W9-BNW-062

Apparitions, Healings, and Weeping Madonnas

Apparitions, Healings, and Weeping Madonnas

Christianity and the Paranormal

Lisa J. Schwebel

PAULIST PRESS
New York/Mahwah, N.J.

Cover: A postcard depiction of the apparition at Pontmain, France, in 1871. Courtesy of the Marian Library, University of Dayton.

Book design by Lynn Else
Cover design by Trudi Gershenov

Library of Congress Cataloging-in-Publication Data

Schwebel, Lisa J.
    Apparitions, healings, and weeping Madonnas : Christianity and the paranormal / Lisa J. Schwebel.
        p.   cm.
    Includes bibliographical references.
    ISBN 0-8091-4223-6 (alk. paper)
    1. Parapsychology—Religious aspects—Catholic Church. 2. Catholic Church—Doctrines. 3. Rahner, Karl, 1904–   I. Title.
BX1795.P37 S39 2004
261.5′13—dc22

                                                                2003019285

Published by Paulist Press
997 Macarthur Boulevard
Mahwah, New Jersey 07430

www.paulistpress.com

Printed and bound in the
United States of America

Contents

For Helen

Acknowledgments

In writing this book I had the great and undeserved good fortune to find myself in the way of extraordinary thinkers and teachers. Each one is a genuine "without whom" this book would not be possible. John Heaney, the leading scholar on religion and parapsychology, introduced me to the topic and gave generously of his wisdom, time, and library. It was John Heaney who clarified the religious consequences—enormous—of precognition for prophecy. Joanne McMahon, an expert in death studies, helped me navigate through a century and a half of parapsychological research, and taught me how to "talk psi." Her thoughtful comments and help on the book were invaluable. Ellen Kadin deserves a medal for wading through the dissertation-speak of the original manuscript. Roseann Bonadia's generous spirit introduced me to Paulist Press. As an editor, Don Brophy is not only a gifted reader, but an all-around classy fellow as well. Barbara Sproul, the religion scholar, essayist, and published poet, listened to it all.

For their unrelenting support, thank you to Isabelle Mayer, Joshua Schwebel, Kathleen O'Shea, Harrolyn Murphy Conway, Mhairi Cameron, Margaret Kay, Sian Lewis, and Ian Martin.

Introduction

On June 1, 1974, at 4:40 P.M., a sudden, massive explosion ripped through a chemical plant in Flixborough, England, taking the lives of twenty-eight people, injuring hundreds more, and virtually demolishing the sixty-acre facility. Four hours prior to the event, a young woman watching television twenty-three miles away reported witnessing a news account of an explosion that killed several people in Flixborough. She mentioned it to friends staying in her home, thereby confirming the time of the televised report.

In 1867 a man's only sister died suddenly of cholera. Several years later he had an extraordinary experience in which he "suddenly and distinctly became conscious that someone was sitting on my left....I turned and distinctly saw the form of my dear sister." He described the apparition to his parents, relating how his sister had a bright red scratch on her cheek. Hearing it, his mother became very agitated. For she had never told anyone how she had accidentally scratched the face of her daughter's corpse during its preparation for burial.

A young boy, suffering from a genetic skin disease for which there is no effective cure and from which children die at an early age as a result of constant infections, is cured through hypnosis. His doctor, aware that skeptics would claim that the cure was the result of previous medication finally taking effect, devised an ingenious plan. According to Hans J. Eysenck and Carl Sargent in *Explaining the Unexplained*, "He hypnotized the boy and then gave the specific hypnotic suggestion that the hard skin would disappear from one arm only. This is exactly what happened. Now, it is simply not credible to claim that previous treatments just happened to affect only a specific part of the boy's body, which the hypnotist then suggested should be cured! The inescapable conclusion is that hypnotic suggestion cured this 'incurable' disease."

How should religious people view these events? Are they miracles, direct evidence of God's sovereignty over the world? If, according to Rudolf Otto in *The Idea of the Holy*, the numinous is characterized by eerie, weird, uncanny, wonder-producing experiences, how can we distinguish between ordinary eerie experiences and those that are uniquely caused by the Holy? To be sure, the stories above fill us with awe and wonder; they overwhelm and frighten us, exactly as Otto describes the effect of the Holy. But in that case should we interpret the factory explosion vision as a sign from God, a divine warning to be interpreted along with other such warnings? Is the apparition of the sister evidence of life after death, as Jesus promised? Should we ask why, if hypnosis cures incurable diseases, aren't more oncologists studying hypnotism?

As we reflect longer on it, we might go in the other direction and treat the examples with skepticism, dismissing them as the sort of tall tales children tell to scare one another. We could scorn them as "urban legends," either completely false or rooted in just enough fact to seem real but exaggerated beyond all credulity. We could easily consider the "vision" as a hallucination, the boy's illness as either wrongly diagnosed or not incurable, and the witness testimony as biased and thereby unreliable. Alternatively, we might concede that eerie, uncanny events do occur. At the same time, however, we could still believe they have a perfectly reasonable explanation—if only people would try hard enough to find it. The problem is that people don't try hard enough; they claim God is behind whatever they don't understand. The stories are nothing more than hope, expectation, and wishes dressed up as facts.

Faced with these and similar unexplainable events, what is the believer to think? Is there no middle ground between miracles and "tall tales"? Where can Christian believers turn to make sense of it all?

In *The Dynamic Element in the Church*, the German theologian Karl Rahner insists that the belief that God acts personally in history is not merely a peculiar feature of medieval spirituality, but is one that, even in the present day, cannot be seriously doubted. For, according to Rahner, "without that conviction, belief in a free revelation by his Word, in the sacred history of redemption, of the living personal God, is impossible." To deny that the divine can immediately reveal itself in the concrete historical situation is, in effect, to deny Christianity itself.

What is the nature of divine activity? Is God limited to operating through secondary causes only? What are we to make of events like visions, revelations, and extraordinary physical phenomena that appear to involve special, direct acts of God? What does it mean to say that God acts directly in the world? Do these acts constitute a special category of divine activity separate from and in addition to God's "ordinary" activity? How are special acts of God identified? Do they require interventions in or suspensions of the laws of nature? And what purpose does God have in these "special acts"?

Theologically, special acts of God generally fall within the framework of mystical experience that serves as evidence of

God's favor, proof of divine reality, or as manifestations of the divine will. Special acts refers to those events and experiences that are commonly distinguished from God's normal sustaining and conserving activity in the world. Special acts are held to exceed natural and human capacities; they are powers reserved for God alone. As a result, if and when such events occur, they point directly to their divine origin. While mystical experience itself may be understood to be a special act of God, the term is used here in connection with the external physical phenomena of mysticism, with visions, prophecies, and miracles: events in which God is perceived not only to "appear from behind the screen" of second causes, but also does so in a dramatic and, frequently, public way.

Rahner gives four reasons why theological analysis—critical, open-minded reflection on issues of importance to committed Christian living—is necessary for special acts. The first and overriding reason concerns the importance of experience for the life of faith. Too often, Rahner says, the experiential ground of faith is lost, or devalued in favor of intellectual representations and doctrinal formulations.

The point here is that the loss of the explicit experience of transcendence is not merely the loss of a side benefit or fringe adornment to faith, or an extra "aid" for the believer who is not comfortable with concepts and ideas (an aid with which the more intellectually sophisticated believer can dispense). More fundamentally, Rahner says, estrangement from the experience of transcendence results in the separation of faith from its originating and sustaining source. In this regard, special events like visions, prophecies, and miracles are distinct and traditional parts of the experience of grace.

Second, Rahner understands that although many alleged special acts of God are of a dubious character, others are more credible, and the fact that genuinely pious people are increasingly paying attention to them shows that they raise issues warranting serious consideration. This does not mean that each claim requires investigation, but rather, that taken as a whole, these events cannot be dismissed as insignificant. Third, the popular mind associates mysticism almost exclusively with special acts of God. One unfortunate consequence of this, Rahner observes, is the belief that these events have a higher sacred value than other experiences of God. Where God is found in spectacular external effects and emotional highs, the genuine mystical experience of God available in everyday life, in ordinary acts of faith, hope, and love, and in the sacraments fades into the background. This position is typified in Desmond Seward's *The Dancing Sun*, an account of his journeys to miracle shrines in search of his lost faith. Seward, a writer of historical biographies, found his faith waning and "lukewarm." His doubts vanished, however, in a "comforting euphoria" at Medjugorje, a Marian pilgrimage center in the former Yugoslavia. When the high wore off, Seward traveled to other miracle shrines throughout eastern and western Europe to "recapture" the feeling "that I might find a more lasting escape from my doubts." Reflection would lead Seward to appreciate the "miracles" available any day of the week in his daily life without leaving his neighborhood. For Christian faith, God's creating, sustaining, and preserving activity is manifest at every moment in every situation—doing laundry, washing dishes, hauling garbage, eating breakfast, waiting in traffic—if we are only willing to pay attention. Since all is of God, the very structures of reality reveal this:

What is not God does not have to move over to make room for God. Miracles are here and now, close and personal. We don't need to change locations to experience a miracle; we can stay put and think about breathing. That we breathe, that our lungs take in and expel air in a regular constant rhythm whether we notice or not, is surely one of God's greatest miracles. If one does not find breathing spectacular enough, one can always try not breathing.

Moreover, even when we look for overt special manifestations of the sacred, what is more wondrous than what Christians believe takes place in the bread and wine? The challenge for Seward and for us is to receive every communion as first communion—filled with a love, joy, and peace so great that we experience ourselves and the world differently. Seward's view of faith, and its inevitable dissatisfaction, are precisely what theological analysis—and this book—are meant to reexamine.

Finally, attitudes toward and beliefs about special events have implications for a doctrine of God. Where God is primarily sought in external phenomena, there is the danger of an extrinsic model of God's relation to the world—a model that requires God to break into the world from outside. These special effects, when not understood within the larger context of God's original self-communication in grace in which the world is God's own world from the beginning, become, if not the only acts God performs, then at least the most revealing acts.

The need for a modern theological analysis of special acts became urgent in the period immediately leading up to and following the Second World War. In eastern Europe alone Rahner notes over two thousand alleged miracles, and in western Europe more than thirty serial apparitions of Mary were officially investigated by the Church during the same period. In addition, three hundred individual apparitional cases to children were reported. The flood of visions and miracles turned into a deluge of claims of supernatural activity; Christians from the most credulous to the most skeptical were overwhelmed by events. In 1958 Rahner wrote *Visions and Prophecies* to help believing Christians to form judgments about these phenomena. It remains the only sustained systematic theological analysis of mystical phenomena.

To be sure, visions and revelations have a long tradition in religious history. In *Apparitions in Late Medieval and Renaissance Spain*, for example, William A. Christian finds that visions of Mary invariably accompany periods of social upheaval, typically, in times of drought, plague, bad harvest, invasion, and occupation. No less than in 1450 than in 1950, the contemporary scene is flooded with reports of apparitional manifestations and extraordinary phenomena. Ireland, Italy, Spain, Egypt, Czechoslovakia, and the former Yugoslavia, are just a few of the countries in which Marian visions have been reported in the last fifty years. In the United States alone, apparitions, miraculous cures, and other paranormal phenomena including stigmata, possession, weeping and bleeding statues, metals changing color, and "spinning" suns have been reported in Texas, California, Wisconsin, Georgia, New Jersey, Virginia, Arizona, Colorado, and in at least two boroughs of New York City. The events have occurred to Christians across church and denominational borders. In an Orthodox Church in Queens, for example, an icon of St. Irene began weeping during the 1989 Gulf War. Indeed publicity surrounding St. Irene's seemed to trigger a mini flood of weeping icons across the mid-Atlantic region. Further, similar effects can be found in Judaism, Islam,

Hinduism, and Buddhism. Some Hasidic Jews in New York claim that their religious leader can effect miraculous cures; a group of Muslim *tariqas* are said to perform mystical healings; and an eighty-four-year-old Buddhist nun in Thailand is believed to have cured a range of illnesses from cancer to paralysis by touch and herbal medicines.

"Do You Believe in Miracles?" asked the July 1991 issue of *Life* magazine. According to a Gallup poll 83 percent of Americans answered, "Yes." In a separate poll Andrew Greeley found that 53 percent of Americans claim to have had contact with a higher reality.

Once relegated to early Sunday morning worship programs and inspirational pamphlets, the *New York Times*, *Wall Street Journal*, *Time* magazine, and all the major television networks now cover religious paranormal phenomena. Father James Bruse was an obscure parish priest in Lake Ridge, Virginia, until he made the March 29, 1993, cover of *U.S. News & World Report* and the evening news when he began to manifest the stigmata and statues started to weep in his presence. No less an icon of popular culture than *People* magazine runs pieces on saints, angels, miracle cures, and people who claim to communicate with spirits, including an article on Father Bruse. The interest in and frequency of religious mystical experiences both reflects and contributes to the general popularity of paranormal phenomena as a whole. Whereas ten years ago there might have been an occasional television special on miracles (e.g., *Secrets of the Unknown: Miracles and Visions* or *Miracles and Other Wonders*), today the channels are clogged with prime-time series featuring one or another aspect of the paranormal: *It's a Miracle; Sightings; Beyond Reality; Encounters with the Unexplained; Beyond Chance; Unsolved Mysteries; Mysteries, Magic, and Miracles;*

Haunted History; Haunted Houses; Crossing Over. Specials focusing on particular topics, like *Stigmata: Wounds of Mystery* and *Tortured Spirits, Tormented Souls* compete for viewers alongside of fictional programs with paranormal premises such as *Mysterious Ways* in which two characters investigate a different "miraculous phenomenon" each week. Then there's the self-explanatory, *Buffy, The Vampire Slayer.* The huge following of programs with such widely different sensibilities as the dark, anxiety-producing *X-Files* and the warm, feel-good coziness of *Touched By an Angel* witness to the range and depth of the public fascination with all things paranormal.

Unfortunately, these programs rarely distinguish between the religious and the paranormal. Instead, they tend to jumble visions, strange noises, healings, spoon bending, ghosts, near-death experiences, UFOs, stigmata, and Stonehenge together without much sense of the differences in type, origin, and significance of these phenomena. In fact the term *miracle* is rapidly becoming synonymous with "paranormal event," losing almost all of its specifically religious character. It is worrisome to the truly religious person that, as a consequence, any paranormal event by virtue of being paranormal is being interpreted as a special act of God.

In the introduction to *Visions and Prophecies,* Rahner remarks that it should be no surprise that in difficult times people not only need God's word, but also seek out those who claim to receive it. Rahner speaks to our own situation when he writes:

> Such "credulity" need not necessarily be suspect merely because it is induced by the anguish of existence. For why should this anguish serve only to agitate man, grubbing up from the dark depths of his

heart nothing but specters and wish-dreams? Why should it not also render him more receptive to the true message from above, to which the comfortable and self-satisfied turn a deaf ear? Both things are possible.

Clearly, the concerns of believers regarding visions and revelations—which ones are authentic and what is the appropriate response to them—are the same today as they were in 1950, or indeed in 1450. The central issue was, is, and will be discernment. Rahner goes right to the heart of the matter when he says, "Since, then, all this is possible, it becomes a matter of great importance to recognize what it is in a particular case that answers the cry of the tormented heart: the empty echo in which, all unawares, one hears only oneself, or the answer in which God is perceived." If discernment is the central feature of the theology of special acts, then integrating the wisdom of the tradition with modern methods and discoveries is the key to discernment.

To be sure the practice of consulting disciplines outside of theology is itself part of the traditional process of discernment. In the eighteenth century Pope Benedict XIV formalized this practice in his four-volume treatise *De Beatificatione Servorum Dei et De Canonizatione Beatorum (On the Beatification of the Servants of God, and of the Canonization of the Blessed)*. Benedict, who developed his interest in and expertise on the subject in his twenty years as a consultant to the Vatican Congregation of Rites (the office concerned with establishing the heroic virtue of proposed candidates for canonization), maintained that in every case where supernatural agency is alleged, the investigator must scrupulously exhaust all possible explanations by natural causes. Benedict himself took a practical and empirical approach in his own investigations. One story about him, recounted by Renée Haynes in her biography of Benedict, *Philosopher King*, in particular illustrates the kind of attitudes required in this area.

While still only a junior in the Congregation of Rites, Benedict (then Prosper Lambertini) was sent to assist in the examination of an elderly nun who was believed, by her convent and the Cardinal Protector of her order, to live without eating. In the course of questioning everyone from the prioress to the kitchen staff, it appeared that the nun had eaten nothing for a month. After the nun had been examined, Benedict asked his senior if he might put a question to the nun that had not yet been raised, "and on being given leave to do so said point blank: 'Mother do your bowels open every day?' Though much taken aback at this indelicacy, she answered firmly, 'Yes, of course.' He pointed out that this would be impossible if she had nothing in her stomach, the inquiry was reopened, and the story was shown up as a complete fabrication, intended to give the convent publicity and alms."

Benedict was widely read and since childhood had a great interest in the natural sciences. In preparing his opus he consulted not only previous works on canonization, but also archaeologists, astronomers, doctors, historians, lawyers, philosophers, physiologists, and zoologists. Benedict solicited from the Academy of Science in Bologna a report on fasting and miracles, and included it in full in an appendix.

As a result of his work at the Congregation of Rites, Benedict developed extensive knowledge of parapsychological capacities, including telepathy, precognition, and psychokinesis—which he observed were frequently, and erroneously accepted as evidence of advanced spiritual development. Thus, Rahner's view that "an adequate study of the relationship between mystical and parapsychological phenomena" is at once "still lacking" and also "one of the most important presuppositions for a theology of mysticism" reflects a line of inquiry that goes back to Benedict and beyond. Such a study is essential to discerning which events and experiences thought to be producible only by God, may in fact be explained by natural parapsychological abilities. A discussion of parapsychological phenomena does not mean God is not at work in mystical experiences; rather, it will point out the nature of God's activity in them.

In this book we continue that tradition by undertaking a study of the relationship between mystical and parapsychological phenomena in the areas of visions, miracles, healing miracles, and prophecy. Chapter 1 provides a more detailed look at the background and the points of intersection between mystical and parapsychological phenomena. Chapter 2 explores the relation between religious visions and apparitional experiences. Nonhealing miracles are examined in chapter 3, in light of research in psychokinesis. The relation between prophecy and precognition will be explored in chapter 4. Chapter 5 examines the traditional criteria for discernment of genuine visions. Finally, chapter 6 looks at healing miracles from the twin perspectives of psychoneuroimmunology (the study of the relationships between psychological, neurological, and immunological factors in health) and biological psychokinesis.

The positions the book takes draw from a wide variety of sources in the disciplines of theology, parapsychology, psychology, psychoneuroimmunology, sociology, and history. Every effort has been made to reference the appropriate sources within the body of the text. Were all of the sources included in individual footnotes this would have been a much different book for a much different audience. However, the reader is directed to the bibliography where full references are gathered collectively; they are strongly recommended as continuing reading material. If I have overlooked proper acknowledgment for any of the material used, I would be most grateful for that information.

The aim is to develop criteria for discernment and apply them to relevant case studies, especially the mystical phenomena associated with the Marian visions at La Salette, Lourdes, Pontmain, Beauraing, Banneux, Fatima, Garabandal, and Medjugorje. Sandra Zimdars-Swartz, a noted expert on Marian visions, observes that paranormal events are "an important but as yet little-studied aspect of Marian apparitions." This work responds to this need and provides an at least "adequate study" of mystical paranormal phenomena.

1.
Mysticism and Parapsychology

Why should the natural parapsychological powers of telepathy, clairvoyance, psychometry not be able to apprehend religious objects, just as the "normal" powers of a religious person do, and thus occasion acts of religious value? And why should not such acts be taken as graces of God?

Karl Rahner makes these observations in *Visions and Prophecies*, his extended discussion of public and private revelations. A thinker who transcends categorization, Rahner is widely acknowledged as one of the preeminent figures in modern Christian theology. In a life that spanned the twentieth century (1904–84), the German Jesuit lived through two world wars and other less global conflicts, the rise of communism and of the Berlin Wall, the atom bomb, psychoanalysis, the birth control pill, nonstop air travel between Germany and Japan, rockets to the moon, and satellite telecommunication. As a result of his experiences he developed a "universalistic" theology whose wide-ranging systematic approach is laid out in two-dozen books, twenty-three volumes of collected essays, aptly titled *Theological Investigations*, and is reflected in key documents of the Second Vatican Council. In contrast to the image of the aloof theologian writing from and for the ivy-covered academy, Rahner was never interested in theology for its own sake; rather, in *Faith in a Wintry Season* he claims, "behind everything I have done there stands an immediate pastoral interest." The purpose of his work, Rahner reiterates in *Theological Investigations Vol. 22*, "is to clarify those individual questions that modern readers are interested in better understanding." Part of the fulfillment of that purpose is the series on disputed questions *(Quaestiones Disputatae)*, each volume of which responds to a subject of particular concern to lay Christians. *Visions and Prophecies* is the tenth volume in the series. In the introduction Rahner makes clear that his aim in the book is to "help believing Christians" form judgments about these phenomena.

Rahner believes that natural parapsychological powers must be considered as part of the process that makes judgments. Although he is not the first or only theologian to refer to parapsychology in connection with mystical phenomena like apparitions, prophecies, miracle cures, weeping statues, and anomalous aerial phenomena (e.g., spinning suns), he is the only one to call for a reappraisal of previously authenticated revelations on the basis of modern scientific knowledge of parapsychology. He has argued that parapsychological investigation, far from being reductive, is crucial to a complete and nuanced appreciation of God's presence to and care for humankind. Indeed, in as much as the world is God's own creation—if it is fundamentally in and of God—any aspect of the world, including parapsychological powers, can be a medium for the transcendental experience of God. So the phenomena of stigmata and "weeping statues" that occurred in 1993 in Lake Ridge, Virginia, to Father James Bruse could be wholly explained by psychokinesis (see chapter 3). And yet, to the extent that it led Father Bruse to deepen his commitment to the Church, it could also be taken as a "grace of God."

This book takes Rahner's views on parapsychological powers as its touchstone. It develops them in light of contemporary research, applying them to specific revelations, and expands on them to consider parapsychological powers as an aspect of divine activity. The first step in the process is to define our terms. ✓

What Is Mysticism?

In the *Dictionary of Theology*, Rahner defines *mysticism* as "an experience, the interior meeting and union of a man with the divine infinity that sustains him and all other beings" and also as "the attempt to give a systematic exposition of this experience, or reflection upon it." The possibility of mystical experience, he says, is rooted in the interpersonal relation between God and the world in grace.

If grace is God's gift of his own creating, sustaining, loving self to the world as well as our awareness of and response to that gift, then mysticism is the heightened, radical, consciousness-transcending form of this awareness and response. Rahner speaks of modes or stages of the awareness of grace that correspond to an expanded knowledge and appreciation of God's complex, intricate, multidimensional, all-encompassing activity. To the mystic, "everything that is, is holy." In *The New Seeds of Contemplation*, the twentieth-century Cistercian monk Thomas Merton wrote, "There is nothing evil in anything created by God, nor can anything of His become an obstacle to union with Him." Merton notes that the only obstacle is our ability "to see and use all things in and for God." Thus between the ordinary believer and the mystic lies a difference not in the quantity of grace, but in the quality of the awareness and response. The mystic is one for whom the relation to God is the explicit, central, intensified focus of consciousness. In *The Cloud of Unknowing*, the anonymous fourteenth-century author instructs the would-be mystic: "Center all your attention and desire on him and let this be the sole concern of your mind and heart....For with your attention centered on the blind awareness of your naked being united to God's, you will go about your daily rounds, eating and drinking, sleeping and waking, going and coming, working and resting."

A possible effect of this intensified focus is the occurrence of visions and other extraordinary phenomena. Rahner says they should be regarded as "overflow" from a psyche that is singularly, willfully, deeply centered on God. For example, St. Teresa of Avila was observed to levitate while in deep prayer. Under the influence of a "divine light" Hildegard of Bingen was able to read Latin; this wouldn't be unusual except that she was illiterate. The vision of the crucified Jesus in a six-winged seraph appeared to St. Francis of Assisi—as did his stigmata—after years of spiritual practice. A feature of St. Catherine of Siena's exceptional piety was her ability to "see into the hearts of sinners"—a habit so developed in her it caused those who had not confessed to head in the opposite direction to avoid meeting her. The twentieth-century Capuchin friar, Padre Pio, exhibited a number of divine "favors" including the bleeding wounds of Jesus crucified (e.g., stigmata), mind reading, prophecy, and bilocation—all of which were recognized by the church in his 2002 canonization as signs of a life that was set on holiness and service.

To be sure these examples don't mean that every mystic has visions or evinces unusual abilities, or even that the content of such visions is consistent, true, or useful. Among the many possible examples of the latter, consider the historical contradictions among the accounts of well-known visionaries concerning the death of the Virgin Mary: Catherine Emmerich places the event thirteen years after Jesus' death; Mary of Agreda says twenty-one years, four months, and nineteen days; St. Bridget fifteen years; and St. Elisabeth Schönau, a year and a half. The number of false prophecies is too numerous to count, but of those that did not come to pass, the nineteenth-century Blessed Anna-Maria Taigi's is notable. During her lifetime, many church leaders, including the pope, believed her prophecies—one of which forecast a cataclysmic period of darkness when all the enemies of the Church would be slain, after which Peter and Paul would return to earth and restore the Church. Many visionary accounts are simply useless. For instance, there are the extensive—and contradictory—detailed visions of Jesus' birth of which St. Bridget's and Mary of Agreda's are only two. Yet all of these examples reveal an association between the deep awareness of grace and the manifestation of extraordinary phenomena. In fact, through the centuries such phenomena have become so identified with mystical experience that they are now regularly and commonly referred to by that term. In this book we will follow that usage and define the mystical as the process and progress of being fully present to God, which can culminate in the experience of union and oneness with God and which may—although not necessarily—include strange and unusual phenomena as part of that progress. Mysticism also refers to the phenomena themselves—visions, prophecies, and other miraculous events that can occur suddenly to persons of no special spiritual development and that do not have union with God as their goal. We will call this *visionary mysticism*, as distinct from a more imageless mystical union.

While this means visionary mystics do not necessarily experience mystical union, they do experience profound personal transformation. Though children at the time of their visions, both Bernadette Soubirous at Lourdes and Lucia Santos at Fatima chose to enter religious orders when they grew up. In fact, as the following story illustrates, it is not necessary to see the Virgin Mary or the sun spinning to be changed by visionary mysticism. A man accompanying his devout wife to Knock, Ireland—where in 1879 a group of villagers had reported seeing images of Mary, St. Joseph, and a bishop illuminated on the gable wall of the local church—was moved by the faith of the other pilgrims, especially by their conviction that the impossible was possible. Sitting inside the church away from the crowd, he began to examine his life and to face the truth about his alcoholism. For the first time he believed it was possible for him to stop drinking. As a consequence, he did stop.

Within visionary mysticism, Rahner follows the custom of distinguishing between visions intended for the benefit of the individual alone (which the tradition calls *private revelations*), and those containing divine messages, instructions, or requests for the wider community (*prophetic* or *public revelations*). In the second group we find many spontaneous cases where the visionary's level of religious devotion prior to the vision was rather ordinary.

It is prophetic visions that require confirming proof of divine origin in the form of a miracle (i.e., a miracle separate from the miracle of the vision itself). Indeed, the tradition is sensitive to the fact that many biblical figures charged with divine missions were not obvious choices: Stuttering was not the only or main drawback to casting Moses as God's messenger. He was also a murderer. Hosea married an unreformed prostitute. David not only coveted another man's wife but also sent the man to his death in order to have her. The Bible also contains a number of public and prophetic careers that were either jump-started by mystical phenomena or confirmed by them, or both. For example, God introduced himself to Moses in a spontaneously combusting bush; later the ten plagues serve, in part, to establish Moses' credentials as Yahweh's representative. Elijah's confrontation with the followers of Baal in the First Book of Kings is a classic instance of the use of mystical phenomena to demonstrate divine reality and to confirm the prophet's position. The biblical story tells how two wood pyres are built and two bulls readied for ritual sacrifice. Elijah challenges Baal's followers to prove that Baal is God by having him light the pyre without human assistance. Baal's followers dance and shout at him to no avail. Elijah gives them extra time, but as the afternoon wanes it becomes clear that nothing is going to happen. Elijah then steps forward, and with the intention of leaving no doubt who the real God is, completely soaks his pyre and the ditch surrounding it with water. Elijah then calls on Yahweh "to let it be known this day that you are God in Israel, [and] that I am your servant" (1 Kgs 18:36). Immediately his pyre ignites in a roaring blaze. A further example of a prophet's authority announced through mystical phenomena is found in the opening chapter of Mark's Gospel when Jesus emerges from baptism in the Jordan and sees "the heavens torn apart and the Spirit descending like a dove on him. And a voice came from heaven, 'You are my Son, the Beloved; with you I am well pleased'" (Mark 1:10–11).

Finally, because we shall be primarily concerned with prophetic visionary mysticism and the miraculous or mystical phenomena associated with it, it is worthwhile to address a common objection to prophetic visionary mysticism: namely, that visions can reveal nothing new because the period of genuine prophecy ended with the death of the last apostle. When examined closely this seemingly reasonable view turns out to be false and un-Christian. To insist that genuine prophecy ended with the apostles is to put an unwarranted limit and condition on God's freedom to act. As a colleague wryly observed, "Do you want to be the one who tells God he can't do it?" More formally, but making the same point, Victor White writes in *God and the Unconscious:* "The task of theology is not to lay down some a priori pattern of how God should reveal and what he should reveal; its task is to bow down in deep humility before the manifold and bewildering variety of what God actually does." According to Laurent Volken, whose book *Visions, Revelations and the Church* appeared at the same time as Rahner's, not only is there no reason to believe that God has stopped communicating, but there is also "nothing to indicate that God has changed the method of revelations since the death of the apostle." He notes that, historically, visions and auditions are God's preferred method of communication.

Rahner says the possibility of postapostolic revelations is contained in the incarnation. Belief in the incarnation, he argues, is belief that God became man in a particular time and place. To say that Jesus Christ is God's definitive revelation is to say that in Jesus we encounter a God who communicates himself in the concrete historical situation, in the here and now. As the Word, Jesus Christ makes known a God who freely, personally, actively, and intimately involves himself in human affairs, and thus can and will continue to have words of guidance for us. To deny the possibility that God can speak to us in our own time and place, Rahner concluded, is to deny the incarnational character of Christian faith.

Once we accept that God reveals himself in works and words (including images), we can turn to the all-important question of discernment: How do we determine if a vision comes from God and expresses the divine will? No definition of visionary mysticism, private or prophetic, is complete without considering the need to discover whether the words heard are God's words. Experiencing a vision of Mary or a statue of Jesus moving is only one side of visionary mysticism; analyzing and evaluating the experience is the other side. Since even those with years of spiritual practice and training can still hear imperfectly (recall Blessed Anna-Maria Taigi's prophecies), those with neither require greater scrutiny.

Authenticating mystical phenomena—discerning which of the strange and unusual events are directly and specifically produced by God—is essential when a vision makes demands on the wider community. The Church insists that for the protection of all, any vision along with its supporting miracles (frequently the only part of the vision accessible to third-party observation) must be thoroughly investigated. Since truth is one, the great thirteenth-century systematician Thomas Aquinas said, there is no relevant science or discipline that cannot be called upon to assist in discernment—including parapsychology. In fact, as the introduction noted, an examination of the relation between mysticism and parapsychology is one of the most important issues in mysticism today.

Parapsychology

Being a newer discipline than mysticism, the definition of *parapsychology* is slightly more straightforward. Parapsychology is essentially the open and critical study of experiences that appear to be paranormal, outside the known laws and paradigms of science. Parapsychology is also concerned with *extrasensory perception* (ESP), knowledge and information that do not appear to be gained through ordinary sensory channels or through the known normal mechanisms for acquiring knowledge. Parapsychologists like Harvey J. Irwin include the word *appear* in the forgoing definitions because they insist it is precisely the task of parapsychology to determine whether an experience is paranormal, the result of processes that are outside the norms set down by conventional scientists. In his textbook *An Introduction to Parapsychology*, Irwin distinguishes "between *parapsychological experiences* that do occur and underlying *paranormal processes* that are mere hypotheses for scientific investigation." As we shall see, paranormal processes have always been part of God's self-communication to us in grace. This means they are part of God's *normal* creating and sustaining activity in the world and, as such, are and always have been a possibility for human experience. Therefore, demonstrating that an event is paranormal still leaves open the question of whether it is a paranormal event in which God acts *differently* from his normal conserving and sustaining activity. Applied to visionary mysticism, this distinction allows us at once to affirm that something has occurred—a vision—and to suspend judgment about its cause. This is especially useful today when, surrounded as we are by peculiar and strange events, we don't want to rush to say of any event, "This God did directly."

Parapsychology is more than just the study of the negatively defined paranormal. Positively, Irwin says, it is the systematic investigation of paranormal experiences themselves, this is to say, experiences in which all accepted means for obtaining information has been ruled out. Parapsychological research divides these experiences into three broad categories: ESP (telepathy, clairvoyance, precognition), psychokinesis (physical phenomena, including psychic healing), and apparitional experiences (a large category that includes the possibility of postmortem apparitions).

According to Rosemary Guiley's *Encyclopedia of Mystical and Paranormal Experience, telepathy* is "the mind-to-mind communication of thoughts, ideas, feelings, sensations, and mental images." For example, I feel the urgent need to phone my friend Sally. Getting no reply, but driven by this strong feeling that she is in trouble, I go to her house and find that she has fallen down the stairs and broken her leg. If I "flash on" or have a mental image of Sally's house or the staircase, this is *clairvoyance*, "the perception of current objects, events, or people that may not be discerned through the normal senses...the seeing may manifest in internal or external visions, or a sensing of images." In other words, clairvoyance does not require Sally's participation in the experience. *Precognition*, "the direct knowledge or perception of the future," would be having an image of Sally falling before it actually happens. ✓

Psychokinesis (PK), according to the *Encyclopedia*, is "the apparent influence of mind over matter." The most well-known example is the spoon-bending demonstrations of Uri Geller. Another example of PK would be all the clocks stopping at the moment of Sally's accident. PK has been divided into micro and macro varieties. Macro-PK refers to effects visible with the naked eye, such as spoon bending and objects levitating. Micro-PK implies slight and seemingly small effects that are not visible with the naked eye and that require statistical evaluation. PK may also play a role in *psychic healing*, "the treatment of illness without a known physical curative agent." If I hold my hands over Sally's (confirmed) broken leg and the break spontaneously heals, this is an example of psychic healing.

Guiley defines an *apparition* as the "supernormal manifestation of people, animals, objects, and spirits…who are too distant to be perceived by normal senses." Suppose, for example, I "see" Sally in my kitchen when I know she is at home and cannot possibly be there. Apparitions of the dead also occur. Had Sally's fall been fatal and I afterward saw her in my kitchen, this would be an apparition of the dead.

Parapsychologists distinguish apparitional experiences from hallucinations associated with drugs and mental illness. Irwin notes that in apparitional experiences the subject or "percipient" receives new and usually true information; the subject nearly always knows the object or "referent." More than one person can experience apparition scenes. For example, if my husband and I both saw Sally in the kitchen at about the time she fell down the stairs. By contrast, in psychotic or drug-induced visions new and true information is generally not gained; the referents are mostly unidentifiable or known not to exist. In addition, a drug-induced vision cannot be shared.

In the next chapter, the relation between visionary mysticism and apparitional experiences will be explored in more detail. Here we merely want to establish that "visions" are apparitional experiences. Guiley's definition of an apparition applies equally to visions. In chapter 2 we will look at the claims by some mystics that the apparition figure is physically present and apprehended through ordinary sense channels. Although anyone who sees an apparition can be said to be having a vision, the term is generally reserved for apparitional experiences in which either the percipient (subject), referent (object), or both, are religious or where the experience takes place in a religious setting. We will use "vision" and "apparition" interchangeably, speaking of "religious apparitions" and "visions of deceased spirits," all the time keeping in mind that the divine origin of an apparition must be proved and is not automatically conferred through the use of the term "vision."

Seeking a term to include both ESP (telepathy, clairvoyance, precognition) and PK, two English psychologists, Robert Thouless and W. P. Weisner suggested the word *psi*, the twenty-third letter of the Greek alphabet. Irwin likens the "use of psi to denote the unknown in much the same way as the letter X represents the unknown in an algebraic equation." Psi is now popularly used as an umbrella term for virtually all paranormal phenomena and experiences.

We cannot stress enough that the manifestation of psi is no more evidence of special divine activity than the capacity for extrasensory perception is proof of holiness. Uri Geller, of spoon-bending fame, currently uses whatever psi abilities he has to advise clients on financial investments. While this may be a good service, especially if he is successful, it is hardly a spiritual perfection.

The Catholic Church has long recognized the existence of psi, and holds that manifestations of it are morally neutral. We are not the first to notice that for every public claim of a miracle, the same paranormal phenomena appear in nonreligious contexts across the general population, even to confirmed atheists. Such appearances are more frequent, and in many cases more spectacular, than among their religious counterparts. For this reason the Church has been engaged in distinguishing those that have religious significance for nearly five hundred years. This position led Pope Benedict XIV (1675–1758) to reaffirm the rule of Gregory IX (1170–1241) that visionary experience is not sufficient, on its own, to promote the cause of a candidate for beatification and canonization. Both held that visionary experience occurred across the moral spectrum, to good and bad people alike. Regarding the prospect of beatification for Joseph Cupertino, a seventeenth-century monk, popularly known as the "Flying Monk" for his ability to levitate, Benedict was initially opposed. Benedict understood that paranormal phenomena could appear in religious contexts to religious people without thereby adding any spiritual depth to their lives. Only after it was shown that Cupertino had lived a holy and virtuous life and had inspired others to religious service, did Benedict agree to beatify him in 1753. Many of Benedict XIV's own observations about psi are affirmed by modern investigators. Such phenomena occur to all kinds of people, not just mystics or saints; visions are more likely to occur to people while asleep, and they often appear symbolically.

Karl Rahner considers parapsychological explanations as, at least, "proximate causes" of visionary phenomena—even in those who are practiced in discernment. For example, in the sixteenth-century Teresa of Avila had a horrifying vision of the death of a group of people. Teresa later discovered that on the same day as her vision forty Christians—one of them her cousin—were martyred in Brazil. Rahner maintains that Teresa's vision was clairvoyant.

Does Psi Exist?

It is beyond both the intent and scope of this book to provide a detailed account of the history and development of parapsychology. We will confine ourselves here to establishing the scientific grounds for asserting the existence of psi and the validity of parapsychology as a discipline to investigate psi. The English psychiatrist Donald J. West observes that the criteria for evidence in parapsychology are much stricter than those for science in general, and Gardner Murphy, past president of the American Psychology Association, in *The Challenge of Psychical Research* argues that "if there were one-tenth of the evidence in any other field of science that there is in parapsychology, it would be accepted beyond question."

Richard Broughton, former Director of Research at the Institute for Parapsychology in Durham, North Carolina, in his book *Parapsychology* claims that the disagreements over parapsychology have as much to do with the temperament of scientists as it does with the actual facts. "Fundamental to the controversy are the *claims* of parapsychology....If these claims are correct, then the existing world view that science gives us will have to be modified—the so-called laws of physics will have to be re-written. Of itself this should not be controversial....This is called scientific progress." But change does not come easily. "The prevailing scientific view will not give in easily to a challenger, and the battle is waged not only with data and reasoned debate but also with ridicule and scorn, censorship and denial, and just about every other rhetorical and political tactic." However, this situation is slowly changing. Among the general public, Broughton observes, parapsychology is not a controversial science; most people either accept the reality of ESP or have themselves had a psychic experience. The number of scientists who now think that "ESP is 'an established fact' or that ESP is a 'likely possibility' has climbed from a low of 8 percent in 1938 to highs of 67 percent and 75 percent in two large surveys conducted in the seventies."

Although the Parapsychological Association was admitted into the American Association for the Advancement of Science in 1969, parapsychology received further acceptance by the scientific community in 1990 when the editors of the standard college textbook *Introduction to Psychology* included a section on psi phenomena in its index of orthodox topics in psychology.

What pried open the gateway to this official recognition was a new method of presenting and evaluating data: *meta-analysis*. Because effects that some believe to be directly caused by God can, in fact, be attributed to natural human psi abilities, it will be useful to look more closely at the role of meta-analysis in establishing the existence of psi—beyond a reasonable doubt.

Meta-Analysis

Meta-analysis is a technique used by scientists to strengthen the statistical power of experiments. In research involving statistical percentages there is a fundamental connection between the amount of data collected and the ability to detect an effect. Thus Broughton explains, meta-analysis involves collecting every study done (whether successful or not) on the target hypothesis, based on the premise that "the more data that can be combined, the stronger the conclusions of the meta-analysis. From this mass of differing results, meta-analysis is capable of extracting a simple yea or nay to a given effect." Meta-analysis "can provide even more meaningful overviews of a particular research area." For a controversial area of science, the results of a meta-analysis can be invaluable.

In 1985 the parapsychologist Charles Honorton applied the methods of meta-analysis to his ganzfeld experiments regarding telepathy. The *ganzfeld* technique involves placing the subject in a mild state of sensory deprivation to remove all distractions and relax the subject's mind so that if there is any psi ability present it will have a better chance of coming through. Honorton followed the two principal techniques of meta-analysis. First he located all of the ganzfeld studies. Then, using the blocking process, he grouped the studies according to the differences in scoring methods, laboratories, number of experimenters (to show that the results were not the work of just one or two researchers working together), and relative dates of publication. Allowing for these and other variables, 43 percent of the experiments yielded significant results indicating the presence of telepathy. The odds against that result arising by chance are greater than one-billion-to-one.

Meta-analysis techniques have also been applied to studies in PK and precognition, two areas also relevant to the theology of mysticism. In 1989 two Princeton University scientists, Dean Radin and Roger Nelson, one a research psychologist and the other an engineer, published the results of their meta-analysis of micro-PK experiments. This was the largest meta-analysis of micro-PK research ever undertaken, tracking "152 reports describing 597 experimental studies and 235 control studies ...from 68 investigations" on the influence of mind on micro-electronic systems.

According to Radin and Nelson, "unless critics want to allege wholesale collusion among more than sixty experimenters or suggest a methodological artifact common to nearly six hundred experiments conducted over nearly three decades, there is no escaping the conclusion that micro-PK effects are indeed possible."

Finally, laboratory studies of precognition involving forced-choice testing in card experiments had been going on for more than fifty years when Honorton and his colleague

Diane Ferrari began to examine them in 1989. One of the most significant aspects of the meta-analysis was the extent of the database available. Limiting themselves to English-language publications alone, Honorton and Ferrari found 309 studies conducted by 622 different investigators involving over 50,000 subjects in nearly two million trials. After blocking and grouping the studies, "30% of the studies were statistically significant (where 5% is expected by chance)." He asked, "Is there an overall effect?" The answer is yes. Meta-analysis of forced-choice testing reveals that precognition is a "stable and highly significant effect."

Meta-analysis has looked at telepathy, PK, and precognition in terms of experiments that can be repeated in a laboratory setting, yielding statistically significant results. Clearly, these experiments are crucial to studying and verifying psi phenomena. However, since visionary mysticism (e.g., visions, prophecies, weeping statues, miracle healings) involves effects in concrete situations, it is worth looking at the evidence provided by spontaneous cases. This is important not only because psi is more purposive here, and has a convincingness of its own, but also because it is these concrete, actual cases that laboratory psi was designed to explain in the first place.

Spontaneous Cases

In *The Medium, the Mystic, and the Physicist*, Lawrence LeShan described an experience that convinced him of the reality of psychic phenomena. In 1963 a woman whose husband had disappeared after inexplicably checking out of his hotel room while attending a conference contacted LeShan. LeShan went to see the psychic, Eileen Garrett, with whom he had been working, without telling her why he wanted the appointment. "When I arrived at her office we went into the room without saying one word about the problem. After she was in a trance, I told her two sentences: 'A man has disappeared; his wife is very worried. Can you help?' She fingered the scrap of cloth [the wife had sent LeShan a scrap from one of her husband's shirts] and presently said, 'He is in La Jolla. He went there due to a psychic wound he suffered when he was 14 years old and his father disappeared.'" Upon telephoning the wife, LeShan learned that her husband's father had deserted the family when her husband was fourteen years old. When the husband was finally located, it was discovered that he had been in La Jolla on the day LeShan visited Garrett.

One possible explanation of what transpired between Garrett and the husband may be something like the sending and receiving of radio signals. The husband was the transmitter and the clairvoyant the receiver. But the radio wave explanation does not work in every case. To show why, LeShan refers to one of the oldest and most famous cases in the history of parapsychological research.

On December 11, 1911, Mrs. Verrall, a noted clairvoyant, recorded in her journal a paranormal perception she had of a man seated on a bed or sofa in a cold, dimly lit room reading a book, *Marmontel.* The book was not his own, but borrowed. On December 17, she had a second impression of the man reading. She observed that it was the memoirs of Marmontel, in two volumes, bound in leather with an old binding, and that it was, indeed, borrowed. She added that someone named Passy or Fleury could also be involved. On March 12, 1912, a friend of Mrs. Verrall told her that on February 20, 1912, he was reading the memoirs of the French novelist Marmontel while lying on a bed by the light of a single candle. The following night, he said, he was seated on a sofa reading the part where Marmontel describes finding a picture painted at Passy, the discovery of which is connected with a Mrs. Fleury. Both nights were extremely cold. LeShan concludes,

> you can work all you wish with radio waves and all the other concepts of our everyday world and every-day science, but you cannot get the radio waves to go ahead in time and be received before they are sent. To explain "damned facts" like this one, you need a new concept, a new definition of man and his rela-tionship to the cosmos.

What are the consequences of the existence of psi phe-nomena like telepathy, PK, and precognition for a theology of mysticism?

Consequences of the Existence of Psi for Mysticism

On the one hand, the existence of psi shows that visionary experience can arise from other causes than religious zeal or neurotic fantasy. On the other hand, the fact of repeatable and confirmed laboratory experiments involving thousands of sub-jects demonstrates what parapsychologists call the "ordinari-ness" of extrasensory perception. Psi abilities exist across the general population regardless of religious affiliation or belief, and this means the mere presence of parapsychological powers in visionary experience does not guarantee its religious charac-ter. To be sure, God can use these abilities to communicate the divine will, much as God works through other natural processes. Contrary to popular belief, however, the manifestation of psychic ability, by itself, is not evidence of God's activity.

Rahner, following the Christian mystical tradition, insists that the burden of proof falls on the person asserting direct divine causality, and before one can do this all natural explanations must be ruled out. As long as an experience can be explained according to a reasonably probable, even hypothetical, theory of parapsychological phenomena, its divine origin is not established. In fact, Rahner claims in *Visions and Prophesies*, the existence of natural parapsychological powers means that "we must disregard many phenomena formerly, perhaps, accepted as decisive proofs of the supernatural origin of visions."*

Between 1961 and 1965 five young girls in Garabandal, Spain, claimed to receive over two thousand visions of the Virgin Mary, identified as "Our Lady of Carmel." Despite the fact that Church authorities have not approved the visions at Garabandal, they still attract followers persuaded by the strange abilities the girls seemed to possess. Indeed, one priest continues to defend the divine origin of the visions (despite the fact that the girls have periodically retracted many of the statements they made about their experiences), on the grounds that only God could have produced the phenomena that occurred there. He and other supporters point, for example, to the seers' alleged ability to correctly identify the owners of objects put into their hands and their knowledge of personal information about apparent strangers. However, if these effects are not tricks or hoaxes they can still be reasonably and plausibly attributed to telepathy and

---

*Unless otherwise noted, references to Rahner's analysis of mystical paranormal experience are from *Visions and Prophecies*.

psychometry (the ability to gain information about people, places, and events through holding objects associated with them).

The "little miracle" at Garabandal deserves mention here insofar as it is the one most frequently cited by promoters of the visions as evidence of their authenticity. The little miracle refers to the seers' claim that they were given the communion host by an angel. In this case, there is a well-known photograph of Conchita, one of the seers, in a trance with the miraculous host on her tongue. One possible explanation is that the effect was faked. Conchita could have concealed a wafer under her tongue or at the back of her mouth, only to produce it at the appropriate moment. Joe Nickell, a former private investigator and professional stage magician who uses his knowledge of magic to write about paranormal phenomena, regards it as a possible sleight-of-tongue feat—coupled with the effects of suggestion. The retractions later made by the girls support his view. Another explanation is that the effect was produced by PK. While this is unusual, the Jesuit psychic investigator Herbert Thurston devotes a whole chapter to the "transference of the Host through the air by some unexplained agency," in *The Physical Phenomena of Mysticism*. Thurston cites a number of cases of a host being psychokinetically transported to people too ill to attend communion. He concentrates on the transference of the host from one location to another in the cases of saints and those whose lives are models of exemplary devotion. He argues that if PK does exist, then there is little better reason for its use then to deliver spiritual nourishment to the sick and weak. A parapsychological explanation of the event of Garabandal gains ground when we consider both that psi abilities are known to be released during altered states of consciousness, such as trances, and also that the girls appeared to exhibit other paranormal abilities (e.g., telepathy and psychometry). One simple test for PK devised by Thurston could have been used at Garabandal: to count the number of hosts in the local churches before and then again after the event, to see if one was missing. (Considering Conchita reported that St. Michael fed them hosts consecrated in earthly churches, this test, while not conclusive, would have made a useful contribution to the investigation of the visions.)

Predictive elements in revelations, where they are specific and genuinely surprising (i.e., when they could not have been arrived at by careful consideration of present events), can be the result of precognition. Consider the case of warnings given to two children, Melanie and Maximin, in a field in La Salette, France, in 1846 by a female apparition figure. They claimed she told them that crops would fail and that a disease would come that would only affect children. Parapsychologist D. Scott Rogo claims the specificity of the two major predictions, along with the fact that the predictions came to pass soon after the apparition, leaves open the possibility that one or both of the children had precognitive ability. This is not the only natural explanation. Nickell disagrees with Rogo. He claims that while the predictions were specific, they were not surprising. Nickell points out that by the 1840s a famine was already sweeping across Europe, and a form of cholera afflicting small children had been diagnosed by the time of the apparition.

Precognition or telepathy would also explain how the children at Pontmain, France, knew prior to the event that the German army would retreat from the area, a retreat that allegedly was not expected. Beginning at dusk on January 17, 1871, only a few miles from advancing German soldiers, a twelve-year-old boy, later joined by his ten-year-old brother, saw in the sky over the roof of his house a beautiful woman. As the evening wore on, three lines appeared under her feet: "But pray, my children," "God will soon answer your prayers," and "My son allows himself to be moved." The second line was interpreted by neighbors to allude to the approaching German army. At both Pontmain and La Salette many took prior knowledge of future events as confirmation of the divine origin of the visions. However, if knowledge of events can be gained through psi, then we shall have to look elsewhere for confirmation of the divine authenticity of the revelations.

Events at Lourdes also provide examples of the importance of knowledge of psi for the process of discernment. The ability to detect underground water sources, or dowsing, is part of an ancient universal tradition and is usually found in people raised in rural, country areas. Some dowsers claim to be able to "smell" water in seemingly dry areas. Bernadette Soubirous could have possessed that ability, albeit unconsciously, leading her to discover the underground spring in the grotto of Lourdes. Her claim that the apparition figure identified herself as the "Immaculate Conception" may bespeak divine origin. Alternatively—since the doctrine was already known and spoken of at the time (a frequently overlooked fact by proponents of the vision)—Bernadette's awareness of the term could be due to *cryptomnesia*, the memory of information learned through normal channels but forgotten, or the result of telepathy. In *The Evidence for the Visions of the Virgin Mary*, Kevin McClure claims that Bernadette was either consciously or unconsciously exposed to the doctrine while staying with her old wet-nurse at Batatare in January 1858, two months before the vision at which the identity of the apparition figure was revealed. The nurse, Marie Lagues, was a devout woman whose brother, a priest, visited the family every weekend. McClure speculates that Bernadette could have heard the phrase from him and projected it onto an apparition figure.

The solar miracle reported in Fatima, Portugal, on October 13, 1917, was the culminating moment in the last of a series of monthly visions that had begun in May of that year. The event is popularly known as the "dance of the sun." Accounts of what happened at mid-day on the thirteenth include descriptions of the sun "spinning" or moving around in defiance of the known laws of physics. The event took place in the presence of seventy thousand onlookers.

On close examination, however, the miracle of the sun presents a number of problems. Not only did all those present not see the phenomenon, but also there are considerable inconsistencies among witnesses as to what they did see. Rahner notes that while some reported seeing a bright yellow whirl, others described the phenomenon as "a thin silvery disc," while still others claimed they saw "something of the lustre of a pearl." Interesting, too, is the fact that despite the presence of hundreds of reporters and photographers at the field, McClure discovered that "there is no photograph of the event that is even vaguely authentic; the one usually presented is actually of a solar eclipse in another part of the world taken sometime before 1917." Scientific records show no unusual meteorological disturbances on the day. In connection with the miracle of the sun, McClure writes, "I have never seen such a collection of contradictory accounts of a case in any of the research I have done in the past ten years."

Still others have suggested it was an optical illusion—the effect on the retina of prolonged staring at the sun—or a collective hallucination. In *Miracles* Rogo notes that despite the attention given to the solar event at Fatima, "it is not unique....There are several recorded cases of high-pitched religious gatherings culminating in the sudden and mysterious appearance of lights in the sky." To be sure, something of an unusual nature occurred on that day in that field. But from a practical perspective it is not clear exactly what happened or what caused the phenomenon.

These and other phenomena suggest that the existence of psi calls for a more actively empirical approach to the study of private revelations. Clearly there are many problems to be overcome, but to find authoritative precedent here we have only to recall Benedict XIV's practical approach in the case of the nun who claimed to live without eating. Empirical investigation does not supplant religious interests but complements them as part of a comprehensive plan for discernment. It is worth noting that the majority of religious visions are recurring, and so readily lend themselves to investigation.

Our ancestors undoubtedly used their knowledge of the world's workings in evaluating revelations. Benedict XIV sought out the best scientific minds of the eighteenth century in preparing his opus on beatification and canonization. In similar ways contemporary believers must take advantage of the scientific knowledge available to them. We already do this when we appeal to the biological sciences in cases of divine healings. It is time to add parapsychology to this list. In fact, as we will see in chapter 6, biological PK has much to contribute to our understanding of physiological processes.

2.
Ghosts and Apparitions

Human beings have reported seeing ghosts and other apparitions since the beginning of recorded history and in virtually
every culture. The first-century Roman philosopher Pliny the
Younger records the story of the philosopher Athenodorus who
rented a house in Athens allegedly haunted by a hideous, chain-
rattling, moaning and groaning apparition. Athenodorus took
the house because he was short of funds and the rent was greatly
reduced on account of its discarnate tenant.

Scientific investigation bears out what anecdotal evidence
has long suggested: Apparitions are common occurrences. In an
Icelandic survey, 42 percent of adults reported having seen an
apparition: 31 percent saw an apparition of the dead, 11 percent
an apparition of the living. Of those who responded in a
Canadian study, 32 percent claimed to have seen an apparition
of a person or animal.* Against this wide background of apparitional experiences, visions loose some of their special quality—
that "specialness" they gain from being considered rare. Given
the widespread reports of visions, it is hardly surprising that
religious believers are among those who say they have experienced them, or that some of the many visions have a religious
character. In this chapter we will compare parapsychological

---

*The primary data in this chapter is taken from Harvey J. Irwin's survey of
apparitional research studies contained in *An Introduction to Parapsychology*.
Where necessary, supplemental material has been included from other
sources, and mentioned accordingly.

research into nonreligious apparitional experiences with accounts from visionary mysticism—apparitions, alleged to come from God, that have been experienced by religious people.

Characteristics of Apparitional Experiences

Duration

There seems to be no prescribed duration for an apparitional experience. According to one survey of the general public, half of the people who claimed to see apparitions said it lasted less than a minute, but a full 20 percent estimated the experience exceeded five minutes. With serial apparitions, the duration of the encounters often varies. Beginning on June 24, 1981, a figure identified as "Our Lady of Peace" appeared to six children in Medjugorje, in the former Yugoslavia. Over the years there have been a range of mystical phenomena associated with the visions, including solar effects, metals changing color, healings, and prophecies. Initially, the apparitions of Mary at Medjugorje lasted for about forty-five minutes each. Twelve years later, they averaged less than a minute. In his comprehensive collection of data on mystical experience, *The Graces of Interior Prayer*, Augustin Poulain reports, "I have heard from several favoured persons that their imaginative visions were prolonged, for some minutes, at least, especially when Our Lord spoke to them." He cites the case of a sixteenth-century nun, Sister Gojoz, who claimed to have had an imaginative vision "that lasted for three years consecutively." Other visions are more fleeting. Some of St. Teresa's visions passed so quickly that they "may be compared to a flash of lightning."

Location

The majority of nonreligious apparitional experiences take place in familiar environments. Only 12 percent of cases occurred in locations to which the subject was a stranger. This is uniformly true with other mystical experiences; nearly all of them happen in places where the person who experiences them feels at home and relaxed.

Senses

Perception of apparitions tends to be restricted to one or two senses. The majority of apparitions (84 percent) are visual, with approximately one-third of them having an auditory component as well. Wholly auditory experiences accounted for 14 percent of the cases. Interestingly, in three separate studies, a significant number of cases were asensory. People reported having an "intuitive impression" of a "presence" close to them, but they could neither see nor hear anything. St. Teresa describes occasions when she clearly felt Christ's presence. "One day when I was at prayer," she wrote, "I saw Christ at my side—or, to put it better, I was conscious of Him, for I saw nothing with the eyes of the body, or the eyes of the soul."

State of Mind

D. Scott Rogo, one of the few parapsychologists to examine paranormal phenomena in religious experiences, states that although apparitional experiences can occur in any state of consciousness, they happen more frequently to people who are asleep. In 1974, British researchers Celia Green and Charles McCreery received 1,800 replies to two newspaper and radio appeals for first-hand accounts of apparitional experiences. On the basis of 850 completed surveys they concluded that even when the subject thinks she or he is awake during the experience, the person is actually still sleeping. The "feeling of being awake" is part of the experience. There is evidence of "false awakening" during the Marian apparitions of La Salette and Fatima (the initial vision)—when the children report being asleep immediately prior to the experience. This is not unusual. Accounts of religious visions from at least the late Middle Ages onward characteristically begin with the seer at rest or asleep and "suddenly awakened."

Apparitional experiences also happen when the subject is clearly asleep, but which he or she experiences as distinct from ordinary dreaming. A student of mine who reports having had telepathic and precognitive dreams since childhood describes the difference between an ordinary and a precognitive dream as "like switching from black and white to color photography." Recounting his strange sleep experiences, a colleague told me: "In a dream, once you wake up you know it's a dream. In this kind of dream, when you wake up you know it isn't a dream."

Even when seers are not asleep, for instance in recurring visions that take place at scheduled times, the seers are generally in an altered state of consciousness. The subsequent visions at Lourdes, Fatima, Beauraing (in Belgium, where beginning on November 29, 1932, and continuing almost daily for two months, five children claimed to have visions of the Virgin identified as the "Immaculate Conception"), Banneux, Garabandal, and Medjugorje all took place after the seers were deep in prayer. Taken together these events suggest that apparitional experiences are more likely to occur when ordinary consciousness is suspended. A counter example that demonstrates the point is the seventh of eight visions at Banneux, Belgium, when in 1933 the "Virgin of the Poor" appeared to twelve-year-old Mariette Beco. It was cold and snowing on the day of the vision, and Mariette was so uncomfortable outdoors she kept bursting into tears. Accounts show that it took unusual effort—ten decades of the rosary and a dozen "Hail Mary's"—for Mariette to establish contact with the vision. It seems clear that conditions made it difficult for her to achieve a fully prayerful state of mind, and this in turn inhibited access to the vision.

Collective Cases

Collective experiences, when several people together claim to have seen an apparition, comprise about 12 percent of reported cases. There are reports of up to eight people witnessing an apparition at one time. However, being present at the scene does not necessarily mean that all parties see the same thing—or anything at all. In instances where more than one person is present, only one-third of apparitions are collectively experienced. In addition, research shows that not all of the witnesses see the same thing. Green and McCreery argue that when collective apparitional experiences are carefully studied, considerable divergences emerge in descriptions of the events. They propose that telepathy among the subjects may be taking place at an unconscious level.

In her book *Encountering Mary: From La Salette to Medjugorje*, the social historian of religion Sandra L. Zimdars-Swartz points outs that inconsistencies and discrepancies among seers in collective religious visions are often overlooked or reconciled afterward by those who promote the visions. For example, two of the three seers at Fatima did not hear everything at every vision. Although the vision of Mary at Pontmain took hours to fully unfold, and despite attracting a crowd while it was occurring, only a very few children actually claimed to see it. Finally, not all of the six seers at Medjugorje see the apparitional figure on every occasion. There is no reason to rule out the possibility of telepathic communication (mind-to-mind communication between the seers) in the above visions, and—in so far as all of the seers in every case were either close friends or relatives or both—every reason to consider it. This also applies to the children at Beauraing, Garabandal, and La Salette.

Apparition Figures

Apparition figures have a number of characteristics in common. The first is that, typically, the figures appear unexpectedly (97 percent of the time) and within ten feet of their subject.

Second, more than 70 percent of recognized apparitions are of people known by the subject to be deceased. The percentage varies depending on the age of the subject. Generally, the older the individual, the more likely she or he is to experience an apparition of the dead.

Third, apparition figures usually enter the scene in a natural way and they generally appear as complete figures. It is unusual for witnesses to see the figure "arrive" out of thin air. Most subjects report that they simply "saw" or "noticed" the figure as if it were already part of the scene before they became aware of it. None of the seers at La Salette, Lourdes, Fatima, or Medjugorje, for instance, report any discontinuity in their perceptual field before or after the experience, and in each instance the figure is accepted as part of the environment. However at La Salette, Mary reportedly came onto the scene as a bright, whirling light assuming the appearance of a person with only the face and arms visible. The children judged the figure to be a woman only by the shape of her hands and face. The figure did not behave as an ordinary person, but rather rose into the air. This also happened later at Medjugorje. During the first experience at Lourdes, McClure reports that Bernadette saw behind a hedge "something white" that had the shape of a young girl. Lucia, at Fatima, reported seeing a figure like a "statue made of snow...rendered almost transparent by the rays of the sun." Jacinta, who was present with Lucia, described "a beautiful lady surrounded by a dazzling light." The examples above underscore the fact that, unlike nonreligious apparitions that are invariably experienced as behaving in a normal fashion, religious apparitions are distinguished—in keeping, perhaps, with their divine status—by an abnormal manner of manifestation. This abnormal manner is part of the normal pattern of religious visions.

The fourth characteristic of apparition figures is that, in contrast to how they first appear, most exit abruptly. This is true in all of the above cases, with the exception of La Salette, when the figure faded away gradually.

The fifth characteristic involves types of apparitional figures. Parapsychological research distinguishes between apparition figures that seem to hang about a place—aimless, disinterested, somnolent, like the traditional "ghost"—and those that appear aware of their surroundings and show signs of motivation and purpose. For example, in 1925 an apparition of James Chaffin's dead father appeared in a dream to tell him the location of an unknown will. The apparition's message eventually led Chaffin to a hidden will that was authenticated by his father's friends who knew his handwriting. As it turned out Athenodorus's chain-rattling apparition, mentioned earlier, was no ghost. It, too, had a purpose. According to Pliny, the apparition led Athenodorus to a spot in the back garden beneath which Athenodorus found a skeleton with rusted shackles attached to its arms and legs. It seems that the moaning and groaning was aimed at uncovering the body, because once Athenodorus reburied it with a proper funeral, the apparition disappeared.

The pattern of Marian visions reveals that they fall into the latter group; they occur for the express intention of supporting a devotion or a doctrine (devotion to the Sacred Heart in the visions at Paray-Le-Monial or the doctrine of the Immaculate Conception at Lourdes) or to establish a shrine or church. In fact, a distinguishing feature of religious apparitions is that there are virtually no recorded instances of religious ghosts.

The sixth characteristic is that apparition figures tend to leave a room through the door. In cases where an apparition figure makes a noise, it is experienced as appropriate to the situation—and while it is unusual in nonreligious cases, some apparition figures do speak (e.g., the Chaffin will case). Interestingly, in none of the recurring Marian visions from La Salette to Medjugorje did the apparition figure speak at the initial appearance. The meaning and significance of this fact for the process of discernment has yet to be given the attention it warrants.

While most attempts to touch an apparition fail, subjects frequently claim to feel a chill or coldness when near one. Medjugorje appears to be an exception: Ivanka reported that she was able to embrace an apparition of her dead mother. And, while apparition figures rarely leave any physical trace, both Ivanka and Mirjana allegedly received a piece of cloth from the Virgin at Medjugorje.

Finally, apparition figures generally appear to be real and solid. The majority are perceived as human-like in stature and appearance. Green and McCreery report that 91 percent of the apparition figures documented in their survey were observed to behave as real persons. They can occlude objects they move in front of and are occluded by objects they move behind. The fig-ures have been observed to cast shadows and have their images reflected in mirrors. The humanlike behavior of apparitions leads people who experience them to assume that the figures are objectively present in the environment. Rahner writes that "the impression can be so forceful that even the saints are moved to form a false judgment." He cites two examples. "At the time when the apparitions of the miraculous medal had become known but not the identity of the visionary, St. Catherine Labouré said with great emphasis to one of the nuns who doubted the bodily reality of the apparitions, 'My Child, the Sister saw the Blessed Virgin, saw her in flesh and blood.'" Similarly St. Bernadette insisted: "I saw her with my own eyes." In fact, questions concerning the objectivity of the image— where, what, and how is it seen—are central to the study of apparitional experiences.

The Objectivity of the Apparitional Scene

Both religious and nonreligious subjects claim that what they see in a vision is objectively present in a spatio-temporal sense, in the same way as normal objects of sense perception are present. The problems associated with accepting this claim— and the inability, based on certain experiences, to refute it—are the subject of intense and detailed discussion within the mysti-cal tradition. Indeed, religious authorities have more than a nine-hundred-year head start on parapsychology in this area.

The Christian tradition distinguishes three kinds of visions. According to Augustin Poulain, an authority on the his-tory of Christian mysticism, the first is made up of corporeal or exterior visions. In *The Graces of Interior Prayer*, he says that these are ones in which "a material being is formed, or seems to be formed, outside of us, and we perceive it like anything else that is round about us." The figure is seen by "bodily eyes" and heard by the "outward ear" like natural speech. Imaginative visions are visions of material objects seen by the faculty of the imaginative sense, without the bodily eye and ear. For example, if my father appeared to me at his funeral but disappeared when I closed my eyes, that would be a corporeal vision. However, if I saw in my mind my father dancing a jig despite his bad arthritis, that would be imaginative. Genuine imaginative visions can be distinguished from pure hallucinations or delusions. The latter represent confusion between physical reality and imaginative intuition. In imaginative visions, the person having the vision is fully aware that the apparition figure is not present in physical reality; it is seen with the "eyes of the soul" not the body. Based on her conviction that Christ never physically returned to earth after his Ascension, St. Teresa maintained that all of her visions of Christ were—without contradiction—both imaginative and real. The third group, intellectual visions, are imageless and wordless, perceived by the mind alone. As such they don't concern us here.

The sixteenth-century mystic, St. John of the Cross, himself both an advanced contemplative and a spiritual director, took a very dim view of corporeal visions. He insisted that they are almost always projections of unconscious personal material and/or pious images, frequently confused with external circumstances. Even when genuine, he said, such visions are distractions from deeper mystical development. There is no harm, St. John counsels, in rejecting all of them.

Rahner takes a practical view of corporeal visions. The issue for discernment, he says, is the extent to which the objectivity of the figure is offered as proof of its divine causality. Just because the visionary scene is "integrated into the normal dimension of sense-perception is no proof of the objectivity of the impression." Rahner suggests that much of the behavior associated with apparitional figures and offered as proof of both their corporeality and divine origin—such as figures moving, touching the beholder, or speaking—occurs also in "natural, purely imaginative processes," during dreams, for example, and are likely the result of the creative subconscious of the seer. Some visions, however, contain material that goes beyond the seer's abilities. Supporters claim this is the case with the phrase "Virgin of the Immaculate Conception" for Bernadette and the "secrets" imparted to the seers at Fatima, Garabandal, and Medjugorje. But Rahner maintains that in such instances the phenomena are either difficult to substantiate or the possible result of psi powers.

Green and McCreery suggest that experiences of apparition figures moving are either the result of "subconscious motor impulses" or some kind of extrasensory psychokinetic force emitted by the subject. They also suggest that the movements of figures as well as the manner in which they are perceived (i.e., the number and kind of senses involved) are largely determined by the seers' preconceptions about apparitional experiences. It is not surprising that modern religious visionary claims include both images and sounds, since the history of prophetic revelations predisposes people to expect both. It is worth noting, however, that some researchers (Alan Gauld, Anthony Cornell, and Ian Stevenson) argue that in a number of cases the activities of the apparition figure could not all be attributed to psychokinesis on the part of the seer. Gauld and Cornell investigated "rapping" noises associated with some apparitional experiences and found the rappings to be a form of coded communication that, when deciphered, constituted meaningful language. They also observed that the movements of some figures were deliberate and intentional. These apparitions, they argue, show an underlying intelligence and personality unknown to the subject.

Corporeality, even if it could be proved, is not the same as authenticity. Assuming the physical presence of the apparition figure leads in many cases, Rahner says, to "impossible consequences." How do we account, for example, for visions of Jesus as a child when he is not one now? How is it that the figure of Mary appears under a variety of different titles, or that apparitional figures are not infrequently perceived in contexts that contradict their heavenly state (as in the case of Christ carrying his cross)? What of those seers who claim to have received information about past events that not only flies against established historical knowledge, but also appears to contradict other visionary claims? "How (without arbitrarily postulating another miracle)," Rahner asks, "Can this naively realistic interpretation of visions explain the fact that not all present see the apparition?" What should we make of visions of angels or scenes "where persons from the other world who possess a resurrected body," appear together with people who do not? Rahner asks, "Do we need here an explanation which would cover all cases? Or shall we postulate an apparent body assumed ad hoc on the one hand, whereas the others are present in their glorified body?" Finally, this naive view raises the question of how a "glorified" body can "physically influence" a nonglorified body, and "whether they also have glorified 'clothes' (after all, they are 'seen' in the vision) like ours."

If the seers insist that the visions at La Salette, Lourdes, and Fatima are corporeal visions—seen and heard with the bodily eye and ear—then they, along with all of the others we have mentioned, must be false. Given the difficulties with corporeal visions, Rahner concludes that although they exist in principle, one cannot conclusively prove their existence in any concrete situation. Generally, authentic visions will be imaginative ones.

In modern terms, imaginative visions involve the substitution of the subject's normal field of vision with an apparitional one. It is simpler to suppose a completely replicated environment than to suppose there are two environments operating simultaneously—ordinary sense perception and the visionary. With imaginative visions the substitute field of perception is so accurate and detailed that the subject is unaware she or he is experiencing a replicated perception of the environment. In fact, there is frequently no noticeable discontinuity between the normal field of perception and the replicated one beyond the addition of an apparition figure. In one case recounted by Green and McCreery, a woman walking in London shortly after the Second World War saw a house bombed to rubble. She passed the house every day, and on one occasion saw a young boy in a red sweater and blue shorts playing on the site. She crossed the street to warn him to be careful, but he was gone. "There was nobody there, and nowhere he could have come from or gone to," the woman wrote. Where she had seen rubble and ruin, she now saw a completely intact Victorian house. "I can't understand it, as I had hitherto seen this [bombed] house quite often. I went back the next day to look again and the [bombed] house wasn't there. I tried the next street in case I had been mistaken, but it wasn't there either."

Why isn't the seer aware of the replicated field of perception? In religious cases, naivete and ignorance of the tradition explain why seers who are not practiced mystics regard their visions as corporeal when they are, more accurately, imaginative. Historically, one hallmark of true divine prophecy is that the prophecy is heard as "interior words." The same hallmark ought to apply to visions—in which case, only if La Salette, Lourdes, Fatima, and so forth are recognized as imaginative visions can their authenticity be considered. We will examine imaginative visions again when we discuss theories of apparitional experiences.

The Typology of Apparitions

G. N. M. Tyrrell is one of the pioneers in the scientific study of parapsychological experiences. In his classic book *Apparitions*, he grouped apparitions into four basic types. The first of Tyrrell's four types is *experimental* apparitions. Experimental apparitions are apparitional experiences in which one consciously and deliberately attempts to project an image of oneself onto another. Though they are unusual, experimental apparitions do not require a religious context in order to appear, any more than they betoken advanced spiritual development or confer special graces on the agent. If psi is as pervasive as parapsychologists suspect, then it is not surprising to find that a saintly individual—Padre Pio, for example—could, and would, cause himself to appear at the side of someone who is in need. Sai Baba, an Indian guru believed by his followers to be a miracle-worker, is also said to have this ability. In one case, Sai Baba promised to be with a woman during her eye surgery. Shortly before the operation began, the woman saw Sai Baba in her room. The hospital staff member attending her entered the room and he also saw Sai Baba. The staff member had no expectation that Sai Baba would appear. At the time Baba was seen at his ashram 340 miles away.

The second group of apparitions is *crisis* apparitions. A crisis apparition is the recognized apparition figure of a friend or relative appearing around the same time that he or she is undergoing some great crisis: at the time of an accident, injury, or death. There is considerable evidence to suggest that severe emotional and physical trauma "prompt" these psychic experiences. As a matter of course during the writing of this book people would ask what I was working on, and when I told them, more than half had their own stories to tell. By far the most common story was a crisis apparition. One story, especially, comes to mind. A woman now in her late sixties recalled that more than forty years ago her father awakened her in the middle of the night. He told her that he was all right but that he had to go away and she was not to worry. Before falling back asleep she noted that it was a few minutes after 1 A.M. It was not until the next morning that she realized how improbable the event of the previous night was—which she was sure was not a dream. How had her father found her? She was not at home and had told no one where she was going. What was he doing? Where was he going? She was disconcerted enough to call home where she learned that her father had died the previous night at around the time that she had seen him at her bedside.

The third group of apparitions is *postmortem* apparitions. Postmortem apparitions are apparitions of a person known to be dead at least twelve hours. Approximately two-thirds of recognized apparitions fall into this category. In his "Six Theories about Apparitions," Hornell Hart concluded that apparitions of the dead are indistinguishable from apparitions of the living. (Postmortem survival as understood here is different from reincarnation. Reincarnation means living again in this world in a different body, while what is proposed is some form of discarnate existence in another dimension of reality.) If postmortem survival is possible, then no matter how extraordinary it appears to us, such existence must be seen as an aspect of God's original creation of the world, and not as a special intervention in it.

Experimental, crisis, and postmortem apparitions bring out an interesting and important feature of psi, namely, that it is largely "need serving." Surveys of apparitional experiences show that they occur primarily in connection with trauma and tragedy; their goal to make known something the percipient does not know or is not consciously aware of knowing. Thus, parapsychologists suggest that, in general, psi is purposive in nature, contributing to the survival and well being of the individual.

The needs-based nature of apparitions is demonstrated in the following experience told to psychologist Benedict J. Groeschel, C.F.R., by a friend who had been a missionary in China during the Second World War. In this extract from Groeschel's book, *A Still, Small Voice*, note how vivid, clear, and unexpected is the apparition figure's appearance.

> Brother Brendan recounted how on May 14, 1943, the Japanese army entered the walled city of Shasi, province of Hupeh, from one direction while the friars escaped through the gate on the opposite side of the city. Escape was necessary because they had been told that the army would kill all the foreigners they found. Brother was quite young, but he lagged behind taking care of an elderly friar. When they arrived at the top of the adjoining hill and saw the path divide, they did not know which way their confreres had gone. They were preparing to go to the right when a figure of a man was suddenly in front of them. He said, "No, go to the left." Brother Brendan

said to himself, "It is Saint Joseph." He was clothed simply in ordinary Chinese attire but was not Oriental. Brother Brendan could not remember whether he heard the man speak English or Chinese, but for the moment he was quite certain that this non-Oriental person standing there in the midst of the Chinese countryside was Saint Joseph. They followed his instructions, and as they ran down the path to the left, they could hear machine guns fire right behind toward the path to the right. Had they gone to the right they would have been killed immediately....Without any other information he was convinced that he had seen Saint Joseph.

Since both psi and genuine revelations are intended to serve and promote human welfare, and since warnings are a prominent feature of both, this may account for, on the one hand, the presence of psi in genuine revelations, and on the other hand, the number of psi experiences that are confused with and wrongly interpreted as divine revelations.

The fourth group are *haunting* or *recurrent* apparitions, traditionally referred to as ghosts. A recurrent apparition is one that appears more than once in the same place to one or more persons. In contrast to other apparitions, recurrent apparitions seem unmotivated and unaware of their surroundings.

While Tyrrell's typology is generally accepted, it does not cover the full range of apparitional experiences. Two of particular relevance are the appearance of paranormal light and the phenomenon of poltergeists. Unsourced light manifestations are a regular feature of apparitional experiences and also form part of the pattern of Marian visions. A bright shining light was all that Bernadette saw initially at Lourdes. In the visions at San

Domano, Italy, Rose Quattrini claimed that she first heard a voice, which seemed to emanate from a bright light. Reports of the visions in Garabandal describe a shining figure in a bright light. Ivanka Ivankovic, the first of the seers to see the apparition of Mary at Medjugorje, saw only a lighted outline of a figure at the first vision. Subsequently, Ivanka reported that the apparition figure emerged out of light and turned back into light at the end of each apparitional experience. People present who did not see the figure nevertheless described seeing a bright light at these times.

A *poltergeist* is a type of recurring apparition. Phenomena associated with poltergeist manifestations include loud noises, object movements, torn clothing, reports of large quantities of water in places where there is no plumbing, stones falling from the sky (inside houses), and spontaneous outbreaks of fire.

While, traditionally, poltergeists were thought to be spirits of the dead, parapsychologists have found a link between poltergeists and the spirits of the living. That is, not all poltergeist experiences are apparitional experiences. Investigators have determined that in the majority of cases, the disturbances tend to center around the presence of one individual—typically, although not exclusively, a child or adolescent who unconsciously produces the phenomena through PK. In one study, 79 percent of poltergeist cases focused on a living agent. Parapsychologists, such as Harvey J. Irwin, have adopted the term *recurrent spontaneous psychokinesis* (RSPK), to describe such cases; they refer to poltergeist "outbreaks" to distinguish these subject-centered experiences from the implication of spirit causation usually associated with the term poltergeist.

According to this view, poltergeist outbreaks "are due to the subconscious use of PK as a release from psychological tension."

"The feasibility of this hypothesis," Irwin says in *An Introduction to Parapsychology*, "is enhanced by those experimental studies which suggest that a person may be able to employ PK *without conscious awareness of either the task to be performed or the situation to which it pertains*" (emphasis added). One study of poltergeist outbreaks reported by Irwin, found that, "41% occurred when there were changes or other problems in the home or the family...15% of focal individuals were known to be suffering from a mental or emotional problem prior to the outbreak, and in many cases such a problem was discovered during the period of the poltergeist activity." William G. Roll, a leader in the investigation of poltergeist outbreaks, in his book *The Poltergeist*, suggests that "what we call poltergeist effects may be 'extrasomatic' (exterior to the body) expressions of psychological stress in the same way as an ulcer is a psychosomatic expression of such stress."

Can poltergeist cases throw any light on visionary mysticism? Assuming that some, if not the majority, of poltergeist cases are subject-centered phenomena, what are the theological implications of RSPK? Is it possible that subconscious PK is responsible for some of the phenomena associated with visionary mysticism? We shall explore this possibility in detail in chapter 3.

Theories of Apparitional Experiences

Before turning to RSPK in mystical experiences, we need to consider some theories of apparitional experiences and ask what explanatory power these theories have in religious cases.

One explanation for apparitional experiences, according to Irwin, is the *survival hypothesis*, a belief "that some aspect of the human being continues after bodily death." This view is similar to the ecsomatic theory of out-of-body experiences (OBEs) and near-death experiences (NDEs). The theory holds that a part of consciousness or personality is able to exist outside the body and is released in OBEs and NDEs. This explains why apparitions of the dead are indistinguishable from those of the living. In both cases a disembodied entity is released; the only difference is that, at death, the release is permanent. (It should be noted that most parapsychologists do not support this theory. Irwin, for one, holds that in OBEs and NDEs the subject experiences his consciousness outside his body; but this is "not a literal event." As a result, Irwin is skeptical of the survival hypothesis.)

Researchers who have investigated the survival hypothesis admit that they do not know what a disembodied entity is (one suggestion holds that it is some kind of energy) or how it is released, but they insist it can only be perceived through psi. Under the survival hypothesis it is naive to consider the apparitional figure as physically present as he or she was in life, and it is naive to maintain that the figure is apprehended through ordinary sense faculties. However, it is appropriate to say that the figure is present in the environment—"seen" through psi. To be sure, the idea of a disembodied entity is widely accepted in shamanist traditions, as Mircea Eliade shows, and is consistent with descriptions of some corporeal visions. The hypothesis eliminates many of the problems associated with holding that; for example, the apparition is seen with ordinary vision, while maintaining the essential claim of corporeal visions—that the apparition figure is experienced as an external entity in time and space. So, in the Chaffin will case mentioned earlier, the survival hypothesis would hold that some surviving aspect of his dead father communicated information (extrasensorily) about the new will to Chaffin.

A second explanation of apparitional experiences is the theory of telepathic dramatization. The telepathic dramatization theory solves some of the problems connected with apparitional bodies. It holds that apparition figures are dramatizations of telepathic contact with another person. Information from the referent is transmitted telepathically to the percipient's unconscious, which then represents it to the conscious mind in the form of vivid images.

One explanation for this dramatic and complex method of communication is that sight and sound are the normal channels by which information is exchanged. In telepathic communication, the mind adopts these familiar mechanisms and creates an apparition to bring unconscious telepathic material to light. Thus, an apparitional experience can be genuine—in the sense that something new is made known—even though the apparition figure is supplied by the imagination.

The telepathic dramatization theory would account for the way apparitions of the dead are frequently seen wearing the clothes in which the subject last saw them, rather than those in which they were dressed at the time of their death, and why the apparition of a saint resembles its statue or painting or a friend or relative of the beholder. Rather than proving that the experience is purely subjective, the resemblance reveals the manner in which the conscious and unconscious parts of the mind cooperate to realize the event. Under the telepathic dramatization theory, Mary's appearance at Medjugorje dressed as a young Croatian woman, or the resemblance of the apparition figure at Lourdes to Bernadette's favorite aunt, or the similarity between the statue of Our Lady of the Rosary at the local church and Lucia's vision of Mary at Fatima, are evidence not that the visions are false, but only that imagination is an element within the total complex of visionary experience.

Rejecting postmortem survival altogether, the super-ESP hypothesis holds that information received in apparitional experiences is actually gained through ESP (e.g., through telepathy, clairvoyance, or precognition). Those who favor the antisurvivalist view, Irwin explains, claim that since "ESP has no limits, the mind has access to all information via ESP, thus gaining any data it may need telepathically and clairvoyantly." In principle, ESP can reach out to anyone, anywhere, without knowing who or where, to retrieve information. The main benefit of the super-ESP hypothesis, supporters argue, is that it does not require any reference to postmortem survival. For example, Chaffin's father could have told him about the will while he was still alive, but Chaffin's conscious mind forgot about it (cryptomnesia) until the dream prodded it lose from his unconscious. Alternatively, Chaffin might have learned of the will through telepathy or clairvoyance from living referents. In neither case is there any reason to suppose a disembodied entity. This means that a seer who claims that God is the sole source of information on the grounds that she or he had no access to it otherwise could instead possess super-ESP.

Assessing the comprehensiveness and adequacy of super-ESP, John J. Heaney, author of *The Sacred and the Psychic*, is wary of its validity as a complete explanatory hypothesis. "The super-ESP hypothesis," says Heaney, "should not be cavalierly forced on every case as if it were of equal value to the survival hypothesis."

Indeed, super-ESP may actually be more incredible than the survival hypothesis. One of the problems with the super-ESP hypothesis is that it involves receiving, identifying, coordinating, and assembling a number of different pieces of information from a variety of unknown sources, in such a way and time that allows the subject to recognize them as parts of one specific picture. This would appear to be a much more complex process than the one it is designed to replace—one in which the seer would possess powers more astonishing than the possibility of a disembodied entity. In the following remarks from "Do Spirits Matter: Naturalism and Disembodied Survival," the philosopher Hoyt Edge claims that the super-ESP hypothesis supports, indirectly, the argument for post-mortem survival.

> However to argue this, i.e., that survival is not proven, we must realize that we have to argue not only for the existence of ESP, but for its existence in a fantastically extended fashion. To say we have no proof for survival is to assert the existence of (super-) ESP. And to say that such ESP exists is to say that we have evidence which undercuts the naturalistic view of man, which in turn, is the main reason for one to reject the possibility of disembodied survival....If it were not for our physicalistic biases, I do not think that we could intelligently argue the logical impossibility of disembodied survival.

However satisfactory the super-ESP hypothesis may be, like the survival hypothesis, it still presumes the gathering of information from an external source. Other parapsychologists have taken a different route in trying to explain apparitional experiences.

The skeptical theory holds that all apparitional experiences are hallucinations and no recourse to paranormal phenomena is necessary to account for them. According to Green and McCreery, an apparitional experience "is totally a product of the imagination and reflects the experient's suggestibility, expectations, needs, social conditioning and unconscious child-hood memories." The main problem with the skeptical theory is that, in many cases, it does not accommodate relevant features such as an apparition's knowledge of information the experient does not possess. In order for the theory to work, relevant features would have to be ignored or distorted. With a number of Marian visions it would mean omitting effects, which, while perhaps not directly of God, are nevertheless real objective-order events.

Conclusions

The telepathic dramatization theory in combination with the survival hypothesis has three implications for religious imaginative visions. First, the theory reminds us that, unlike their non-religious counterparts, the presupposition and goal of genuine mystical visions is the moral and spiritual transformation of the seer, not the acquisition of new information. The apparition scene is a dramatic representation of the effect of the transformation on the seer's spiritual life. Indeed, deep levels of spiritual development may release latent psi abilities which occur as a consequence or by-product of this development, but which have in themselves no religious significance apart from leading the subject to greater and deeper awareness of God's gifts.

Second, there may be some religious visions that are, in fact, only telepathic dramatizations. They may be a result of parapsychological powers, with the religious elements being supplied after the event by the seer. Seers who are not at a mature level of spiritual development and who have no knowledge of parapsychological powers may draw the conclusion that their vision is of God when it is really a matter of telepathic dramatization from some other human person. There is nothing supernatural going on. To be sure, telepathic dramatizations may subsequently lead to moral and religious progress even though they are not produced by or a consequence of religious progress. The genuineness of a vision does not depend on the extraordinariness of the effect.

Third, if there is postmortem survival and telepathic communication between the living and the dead, then apparitional experiences of saints can occur. If the psychic bodies of ordinary people are fully liberated at death, and if apparitions of the dead are generally purposive (giving warnings or revealing important information), then saints are more likely to have reasons for appearing for the benefit of humankind. However, just because an apparition is identified as a saint does not mean a miraculous intervention has taken place. Since parapsychological research shows that apparitions of the dead are natural occurrences, apparitions of saints are not "special" at all, but simply part of God's original self-communication. What they do require is proof. The telepathic dramatization theory offers an intriguing empirical means for proving the divine origin of a vision—by its content.

It can be proven that an apparition figure is truly that of a deceased person only when it reveals information that the figure alone possessed. The knowledge must be such that the seer could not have obtained it otherwise—either through ordinary or telepathic means from the figure while she or he was still alive or from other still-living sources. "Testing" apparition figures to validate their identity has always played a key role in the investigation of religious visions. For example, the location of the underground spring and her knowledge of the phrase "Immaculate Conception" were both offered as proof of the genuineness of Bernadette's visions. "It must be Mary," promoters said, "because Bernadette herself does not know such things." Clearly, though, dowsing and telepathy from living sources could account for her knowledge. Since in practice it's difficult, if not impossible, to rule out telepathy, it does not seem possible that any apparition of the dead will meet this criterion. So the only certain way to authenticate a religious vision (where authentication depends on establishing that no one but God could have produced it) would be to show that it contained knowledge God alone possessed! We will examine this seemingly impossible situation in chapter 4.

Brother Brendan's apparitional experience of St. Joseph rescuing him from the Japanese army is illustrative. One explanation of the experience is that Brother Brendan received the information directly from a surviving St. Joseph. While in theory this explanation cannot be entirely ruled out, the circumstances do not warrant it. After all, there is nothing in the content of the vision that he could not have known through telepathic impressions from the advancing soldiers. Brother Brendan, then, may have unconsciously projected the apparition of St. Joseph, which "instructed" him on the safe route of escape. Alternatively, Brother Brendan's superior could have told him which path the friars would follow, but in his panic Brendan forgot—until his unconscious supplied it by means of an image of St. Joseph. This would be an example of cryptomnesia—the unconscious memory of information learned through normal channels. We will return to the relation between the content of a vision and its divine origin when we examine the various forms of prophecy in chapter 4.

Of all the problematic areas in the study of apparitional experiences, postmortem survival generates the greatest controversy. Before theology can reflect on this problem, more work must be done to determine what the survival hypothesis actually involves. Much will depend on the results of scientific investigation still in its early stages. As a beginning, it is worth reconsidering when death actually occurs. According to Cedric Mims, Professor of Microbiology at Guys Hospital London, "Death is a process rather than a single definable event." Building on this notion, Joanne D. S. McMahon, one of the foremost thinkers in "death studies," proposes that what we conventionally think of as the end of "life" might well be delayed anywhere from three to five days after "death," a period that spans the pronouncement of death to the onset of decomposition. This period corresponds to the time frame for most crisis apparitions, which comprise the single largest category of apparitional experiences. McMahon hypothesizes that these apparition figures may very well be the result of conscious intention on the part of a still "living" person. If McMahon is right, then the number of even potentially genuine postmortem apparitions shrinks considerably.

If postmortem survival extends beyond this period to some kind of "life after life," then problems arise concerning judgment and the "definitiveness of eternity," as Rahner phrases it. These problems need to be resolved. In the meantime, the Christian can be clear on two points: If there is life after life, it is part of God's work in creation, and no matter how many "lives" we have, their end (as their survival) lies in God.

In this chapter we examined various characteristics, types, and theories of apparitional experiences. Now we turn to poltergeist outbreaks, one of the most fascinating types of parapsychological phenomena, to see what role unconscious psychokinesis plays in mystical experience.

3.
Weeping Icons and Other Unusual Phenomena

In "Seances for the Tsar," Thomas E. Berry quotes from the December 17, 1833, diary entry of the Russian poet Alexander Pushkin:

> ...In the city they are talking about a strange occurrence. In one of the houses belonging to the directorship of the court horsestable, furniture took it upon itself to move and jump. The matter went to officials. Prince V. Dolgonsky started an investigation. One of the clerks called a priest, but during the service, chairs and tables did not want to stand peacefully. Various interpretations are going around.

It is tempting to claim that religious physical phenomena are altogether different from poltergeist experiences. But when pondering inexplicable events, a moving statue of the Virgin Mary is no different from a kitchen table turning itself over. Liquid "tears" seeping from a block of wood or plaster is no more, and possibly less, extraordinary than water pouring into a room that has no plumbing source. Most investigations of visionary experiences tend to focus on natural causes, in accord with known scientific laws and paradigms, or, when those have been ruled out, a supernatural explanation. This book offers a third alternative: a natural parapsychological explanation. If there is such a capacity as "mind over matter," then, from that perspective, all these events appear to be similar.

Weeping icons and moving statues present an interesting point of departure for weighing the role of psi. Because such events frequently occur in the presence of particular individuals, in parapsychological terms the focal agent is already identified. Even where the *focal agent* is not immediately identified, one may discover whether a particular person—priest or layperson—is present whenever the phenomenon begins. According to RSPK theory, the agent is often completely unaware that he or she is producing the effect. It is helpful to remind ourselves that more than one person may be involved in producing poltergeist outbreaks. Several people in a church can together be responsible for producing an effect.

A Theory of RSPK and Weeping Icons

With the help of parapsychological analysis of empirical case studies, one can construct a theory of weeping icons and moving statues. First of all, a focal agent or agents unconsciously produces an effect through PK. The effect may continue at the location after the focal agent has left the area, which is referred to, Rogo says, as the *linger effect*. As the phenomenon gains public attention, it attracts crowds of people, one or more of whom is psi sensitive. Not only are the visitors able to pick up on or plug into what has been left behind, but the phenomenon also triggers their own latent psi capacity, causing them to release whatever psychokinetic ability they possess onto the same object or site. A process of *psychological infection* takes place at the sites, whereby subject-centered phenomena produced by one group stimulate similar activity in others. The subsequent release of PK by other sensitives prolongs the linger effect, affects still more persons, and, as a result, extends the phenomenon over time. Since we've already seen that the cessation of psychic phenomena is linked to the gradual dissipation of the linger effect, it follows that extending the effect will maintain or increase the amount of psychic phenomena.

The linger effect helps to explain why apparition sites continue to generate paranormal effects long after the initial event has passed. Over the years the original event is reinforced by psychic contributions from later visitors. Indeed, the more successful the site, the more visitors it attracts. The more visitors it attracts, the more likely it is that there will be sensitives among them. The situation snowballs: The steadier the supply of sensitives, the stronger the linger effect; the stronger the linger effect, the longer the phenomena continue; the longer the phenomena continue, the more successful the site, and so on. In some cases an apparition site may not be successful because the linger effect is weak. Clearly the linger effect is a more efficient explanation of the continuing instances of cures at Lourdes— long after Bernadette's visions had ceased and she herself was dead—than the alternative theory, a multiplication of miracles.

This theory raises intriguing questions. Must the psi capacity released by contact with a psychic field always be in the same form as the original effect? For instance, where PK is operating, does it attract only those who have latent PK ability, or can it trigger different psi capacities as well, such as telepathy or precognition? Along the same lines, assuming that a psychic field is built up and that it acts to release PK in others, must it be directed toward the same object? Some apparition sites evince more than one psychokinetic effect, for instance metals changing colors, icons weeping, water appearing in strange places, and so forth. Given that psi is largely an unconscious ability and therefore hard to control, and that place-centered poltergeist effects do vary, it is possible that, once released, PK can erupt in different directions. So one may distinguish between the original cause of the effect and subsequent manifestations of it.

The linger effect also explains why certain people witness the phenomena and others don't. Some people are simply more sensitive and receptive to psi than others. It's highly likely that some of those receptive to psi are also religious. Can RSPK help to explain some religious apparitional experiences?

Case Studies: Theresa Musco, James Bruse, Ivanka Ivankovic

Theresa Musco, an Italian woman from Caserta, a small city north of Naples, reported having visions of Jesus and Mary from the time she was five years old. From the age of nine she claimed to bear the marks of the stigmata on her hands and feet. It was also said of her that she could "read hearts." Theresa's visions did not attract public attention until February 1975, a year before her death at the age of thirty-three, when pictures, statues, and crucifixes in her home began to drip a liquid said to be blood. The community took this as a sign that her visions were authentic, and she became the center of a following that continues to this day.

Theresa's case points out the enormous impact that phenomena like moving, weeping, and bleeding statues have on the public's imagination. The possibility that subject-centered PK could have produced the phenomena is important because it was the absence of an alternative natural explanation—a lack of knowledge about psi capacities—that resulted in the belief that the effects were of divine origin. That the phenomena were decisive in convincing the community is underscored by the fact that without them, Theresa Musco would have remained as she was before the icons started bleeding: a poor, sick, devout young woman known to have religious visions. However as a result of the phenomenon she became a public figure, and the visions that she had had since childhood were suddenly treated as authentic.

If poltergeist outbreaks represent a means of attracting attention or expressing emotional conflict through paranormal displacement, then Theresa Musco's life fits the profile of an RSPK focal agent. According to her biography, *A Short Story of a Victim*, Theresa suffered from a variety of illnesses and spent her life in constant pain, in and out of the hospital. In her diary she wrote that her father beat her and finally threw her out of the house. Anxiety over living conditions, particularly housing, has been found repeatedly in investigations of poltergeist focal agents. Dispossession was also a factor at Lourdes and at Fatima. At the time of her visions at Lourdes, Bernadette's family lived in an abandoned jail following a series of evictions resulting from her father's unstable behavior. The arrangement was understood to be the last stop before the street. Although not as severe as Bernadette's situation, the Santos family of Fatima went through its own housing crisis. Lucia was taken out of school and sent to work herding sheep because her father's poor judgment (or gambling, as some accounts claim) had forced the family to sell part of their land, and threatened what land remained. Clearly both Bernadette and Lucia had reason to feel insecure about their living conditions.

At the age of thirteen Theresa Musco had a vision in which she was told to consecrate herself to lifelong virginity. Her biographer reports that while in the hospital she had to fight off the "lecherous" advances of a doctor. This corresponds to Nandor Fodor's discovery of a possible subconscious psychosexual component in some RSPK experiences. Theresa saw herself as, at once, a victim and a penitent. She reported that as an adult she regularly felt scourging on her back. In their 1979 book *Poltergeists*, Alan Gauld and Anthony D. Cornell found personal assault to be a feature in 15 percent of the five hundred cases they investigated.

The psychologist Erik Erikson has shown that the middle thirties of a person's life is a particularly stressful period in identity formation. This is the stage of mature adult ego development, represented objectively by taking on professional responsibilities and by beginning a family. In their thirties both men and women begin to experience anxiety over their futures. The period can bring about emotional conflict and depression even for well-adjusted people. For Theresa Musco, who spent most of her life sick and confined to bed, the victim of abuse, unable to participate in normal life experiences or to forge a positive adult identity, it would have been an especially vulnerable time—one that could easily have precipitated an emotional crisis. The level of anxiety and frustration would undoubtedly be heightened by the lack of an outlet for relieving it. According to RSPK theory, the bleeding statues can be a manifestation of and a release from this frustration.

Similarly Father James Bruse was thirty-six when he appeared on the cover of *U.S. News & World Report* (March 29, 1993) as the statues at his parents' home and at St. Elizabeth Ann Seton Catholic Church in Lake Ridge, Virginia, began to weep in his presence, and when he began to manifest signs of the stigmata. By his own admission, he was suffering from depression brought about by crises of faith and vocation. Father Bruse's experiences look like subject-centered PK outbursts reflecting and expressing his emotional conflict. The linger effect would also explain how the statues continued to weep even after Father Bruse left the room.

Only fifteen, Ivanka Ivankovic was the first to see the apparition of Mary at Medjugorje, and it was Ivanka who pointed out the apparition figure to the others. From a parapsychological perspective, the fact that Ivanka's mother died just the previous month identifies her as a potential focal agent. Indeed the death of her mother is a recurring and primary theme in Ivanka's relation with Mary.

These cases bring out another feature of RSPK outbreaks: *object focusing*. Object focusing, according to poltergeist expert William G. Roll, means that repressed turmoil often singles out certain areas or objects that are significant to the agent. One focal agent's unhappiness over her mother's lack of attention expressed itself in her mother's favorite picture repeatedly falling off the wall. Applied to religious cases, object focusing suggests that when religion plays a central role in a subject's life, unconscious displacement of tension will manifest in relation to religious objects, for instance weeping or bleeding icons, and religious figures such as the Virgin Mary.

The similarities between religious seers and nonreligious focal agents are rather broad, because there have not been full scientific investigations of religious seers. Information provided in "official" biographies and autobiographies of seers is suspect owing to the occasions for which they are composed (i.e., the promotion of a candidate for sainthood or the generation of interest in an apparition site). However, when religious and secular cases are examined side by side, an interesting picture emerges. In both, the phenomena usually center on a subject who is under intense stress, either physically, in the form of bodily assault or fear of assault, or psychologically, due to feelings of rejection, unworthiness, and/or emotional conflict. More commonly, elements of both physical and psychological trauma can be found. Dispossession, reversal of fortune, and other forms of severe loss, whether actual or threatened, are recurring leitmotifs in both cases.

In fact the main difference between religious and nonreligious RSPK cases appears to revolve around context. Subject-centered PK is religious when an agent interprets psi effects in light of previously held religious beliefs. So we need to ask what a religious context adds to RSPK experiences. Before doing so, however, it will be useful to take a closer look at the focal agent profile.

Profiling the Profile

Over the last ten years researchers have developed new theories about focal agents. Hans J. Eysenck and Carl Sargent, two English psychologists, have pointed out that, in most investigations, the focal agent is referred to a psychologist or psychiatrist who is usually already informed about the reason for the referral. In such cases there is a tendency for the therapist to find a disorder that will explain the "bad" behavior. Eysenck and Sargent add, "Even if that person [the therapist] doesn't know the reason for the referral (most unlikely) and diagnoses the child as neurotic, the child may have become neurotic precisely because she is being persecuted by a poltergeist!" They maintain that "unless reliable personality tests have been done before poltergeist activity occurs, how is one to know?" In the absence of prior testing, they say, "it is almost impossible to be sure of any picture of personality factors" of focal agents.

The link between subject-centered PK and sexual frustration is called into question by the number of cases that are quickly resolved after only one or two visits from a doctor or researcher. According to Eysenck and Sargent, "unless we assume professional malpractice, it is hard to see how such visits could have resolved frustrated sexuality. They might, however, have done something for the self-esteem of a confused and neglected youngster." Further, the number of middle-age focal agents challenges the link between poltergeist activity and adolescence. This underlines the point that age is no determinant of emotional maturity or success in resolving identity issues.

Attention seeking has long been thought to be responsible for poltergeist activity. (In one study by Roll, a staggering 62 percent of focal agents age eighteen or younger were not living at home at the time of the activity.) The problem, however, is that there are many neglected people, adults as well as children, who do not become centers for PK activity. There are many neglected, depressed, and sexually frustrated people, and nothing unusual happens around them.

Clearly the link between mental disorders and poltergeist activity is neither straightforward nor all embracing. It would be wise to reject any theory that holds that all focal agents are mentally ill. Such a belief is as limited and one-sided as the one it is meant to replace. This does not mean that psychological factors, even pathological ones, play no role in these events. There will be cases where psychological factors are unavoidably present and must be considered. Are they sufficient in themselves to produce poltergeist effects? Probably not. Otherwise, we would expect much more activity than there actually is. In fact, genuine poltergeist cases—cases that defy known scientific explanation—are rare. We need to put psychological factors in perspective as elements within a larger complex of processes at work in poltergeist activities. Doing so will involve a fundamental change in attitude toward mental disorders such as aggression, hostility, attention seeking, stress, anxiety, conflict, depression—all of which interfere with full, positive living. Rather than seeing these states as fixed parts of personality, we need to see them as reactive coping strategies. In *Going on Being*, Mark Epstein, a psychiatrist and practicing Buddhist, says that coping strategies are "self-created" at a very early age; they "spring from a fundamental fear or confusion, a reaction to things being out of control." Instead of regarding these coping strategies in a purely negative way, leading to "outbreaks" of "disruptive" and "disturbing" behavior, they may reveal opportunities for growth and transformation. Coping strategies block a person from facing fear and confusion directly, but, as we shall see, they can also be the means for working through them.

In relation to poltergeist activity, the link with anxiety, hostility, and conflict suggest two possibilities. On the one hand, research tells us that PK tends to occur outside the boundaries of ordinary consciousness. Since coping strategies involve powerful feelings, they may put some people in a state of consciousness conducive to PK. Anyone who has been extremely angry knows the feeling of being entirely taken over by anger. Reason and judgment are overwhelmed: One is insensitive to the consequences of behavior or words. For however long it lasts, anger permeates a person's perspective. Considering what conscious anger does to us, repressed anger can be even more powerful. Being unacknowledged, it grows and intensifies. In this case PK is a by-product of powerful feelings—feelings that, Epstein says, "grab our entire being and shape who we become." In some people we can suppose that these feelings open up access to PK.

To be sure, love and joy are also strong feelings that can overwhelm reason and shape our being. Do they also produce "poltergeist-like" activity? The answer is yes. The difference is that the term *poltergeist*, with its physically violent associations, does not seem to fit where love is concerned. Instead, we might say that the lives of saints and mystics contain reports of what, from a parapsychological view, are recurrent, spontaneous, psychokinetic effects (e.g., St. Joseph Cupertino, whose habit of levitation earned him the title "Flying Monk"). Parapsychologists also have noted the link between RSPK and love. Haraldur Nielsson, a founder of the Experimental Society of Iceland, had this to say in his article, "Remarkable Psychic Phenomena in Iceland," about a case he investigated in 1907: "It should be remembered by the reader that [my colleague] has only described one side of these phenomena and the roughest one, and those were the ones most convincing to him. But the phenomena had also a different side, an amiable one, and I have never met with such loving kindness...." Nielsson concludes that, "if this all originated from the medium's subconscious, then he was a wonderful man." It seems that love can also produce subject-centered PK with effects that are not violent or rough.

Genuine love and joy are not reactive coping strategies. Unfortunately more of us operate from unconscious feelings of unworthiness and repressed anger than from conscious joy and love. It is this sad fact, rather than any inherent link between

subject-centered PK and hostility, that accounts for the emphasis on pathological elements in the profile.

The second possibility is that pathological elements are
present and relevant factors in poltergeist outbreaks even when
the outbreaks themselves are understood as potentially trans-
formative. Because individuals who have had a happy childhood
are likely to be happy with themselves as they are, they will have
no reason to access different states of consciousness to create a
different life for themselves. By contrast, those who have had an
unhappy childhood, who have experienced early rejection or
neglect resulting in feelings of unworthiness, may react or com-
pensate by thinking of themselves as special, as superior. If PK
activity emerges around them and is recognized by others, those
individuals will see it as further confirmation of their superior-
ity. (Roll found that the presence of observers significantly
enhanced the PK effects in 78 percent of cases.) It is important,
however, that the analysis does not end here. Rather, in rein-
forcing the subjects' belief in their own specialness, PK effects
can lead people to become the superior individuals they believe
themselves to be. This means that when approached from a
positive perspective, RSPK can liberate subjects from the overwhelming grip of unconscious feelings. As fear and confusion
recede, subjects consciously experience some measure of self-
control. Examples of this are found in religion.

Historically, and in many different cultures, mental instability is regarded as a temporary stage in mystical and shamanic initiation. In *Rites and Symbols of Initiation*, the historian of religion
Mircea Eliade observes that "In some instances this period of
incubation is marked by serious symptoms.... The future shamans
among the Tungus, as they approach maturity, go through a hys-
terical or hysteroid crisis." Eliade notes that this leads some

scholars to view shamanism as a mental disorder. "But the problem was wrongly put. For, on the one hand, it is not true that shamans always are, or always have to be, neuropathics; on the other hand, those among them who had been ill *become shamans precisely because they had succeeded in becoming cured.*" The future shaman gives suffering "a religious significance and, by the fact, accepts [it] as an ordeal indispensable to his mystical transformation." The key point to remember, Eliade says, is that for the religious person "initiatory death is always followed by a resurrection; that is, in terms of psychopathological experience, the crisis is resolved and the sickness is cured."

Evidence suggests that Theresa Musco, Father Bruse, and Ivanka Ivankovic went on to lead fuller, more integrated, less reactive lives as a result of their experiences. Moreover, from a public perspective, why shouldn't their experiences of transformation inspire others?

Effects of Religious Belief on RSPK Outbreaks

To be sure, a note of caution needs to be introduced into the profile of focal agents. As we have seen, it is important not to associate all poltergeist phenomena with mental illness. Richard Broughton writes in *Parapsychology*, "We must be careful not to 'over psychologize' our poltergeist agents...it is easy to find psychopathology and stress conditions anywhere one looks for them. Now that parapsychologists expect to find psychopathology, it is not surprising that they do find it in these cases." Even the language used to describe the phenomenon—"outbreak," "disruption," "disturbance"—reinforces a pathological profile. We don't, for example, refer to an "outbreak of good health."

It is our contention that where visions appear to be a case of subject-centered PK, the subject's belief that the event is caused by a divine figure can be curative. Although not encouraged, such phenomena as weeping and bleeding statues are generally well received by the public; they are not referred to as "outbreaks" or "disturbances." The focal agent—the divinely favored one—is not generally regarded as mentally unstable. Quite the opposite. The public nature of the phenomena is taken, by the community and perhaps even by the seer, as evidence of the seer's sanity.

The belief that Jesus or Mary or a saint causes a statue to move or bleed, or a tree to flower out of season, or a stream of water to appear, is similar to the belief in nonreligious poltergeist outbreaks that spirit-forms move furniture, cause water to cascade, and so on. The difference is that while in ordinary nonreligious subject-centered cases the focal agent is made aware of his or her role in manifesting the phenomena, in subject-centered religious cases, the seer, believing divine agency is at work, seeks to enter into a relationship with the divine figure. The relationship that the subject (unconsciously) projects and enters into with the divine spirit provides religious PK events with their positive therapeutic effects.

In Jesus, Mary, or a saint, the subject finds a confidante, a champion, a powerful friend to whom all sorrows and injustices can be safely unburdened. In some cases, the subject enters into the relationship so deeply and in such a way that he or she begins to see his or her own pain and suffering linked with and transformed by the divine figure. This not only elevates the subject's suffering from the level of personal to cosmic drama, but also from a psychological perspective the subject no longer feels unworthy and rejected, but rather understood and beloved. What psychiatrist in Mark Epstein says in *Going on Being* about therapy is also true of religion: "People come to therapy [and religion] plagued with a sense of personal unworthiness but propelled by a movement toward wholeness."

Religious PK would appear to be especially useful in cases where the subject has no access to psychological help, is culturally unlikely to seek it out, or when the circumstances that cause the emotional turmoil are unlikely to change—when, for instance, confronting a problem might only create more tension. In such cases, the subject's relationship with Jesus or Mary can fill the therapeutic void. For Theresa Musco, the Jesus that appeared to her discerned her innermost thoughts, listened in a nonjudgmental way to her problems, understood and accepted her, soothed and counseled her, responded and instructed her. The relationship mediated unconscious forces in the only form in which she could completely trust and have confidence.

At Medjugorje, Mary's role as the archetypal mother played a similar function in the seers' lives. Mary was described as the perfect mother, a confidante and friend who is nurturing, patient, loving, wise, always knowing when she is needed, and interested in all aspects of their lives. She counseled and advised Ivanka Ivankovic, the primary seer, on her choice of career, and approved her decision to marry. Mirjana Dragicevic regarded Mary as her own mother and best friend. Vicka Ivankovic left school and returned to Medjugorje because, she claimed, Mary told her that she was concerned that Jakov Colo, the youngest seer, should not be left alone. As the good mother, Mary altered the times she appeared to Ivan Dragicevic so as not to disturb his schedule of classes at the seminary.

Unaware that they are the causes of the phenomena, seers will regard the manifestations as validation of their relationship with the divine. The phenomena reveal the emotional intensity of the relationship and the degree to which the subjects have invested themselves in it. Moreover, the validation is empowering. The favor and confidence of a divine figure can boost the subject's own self-esteem, enhancing feelings of self-worth and self-respect. Father Bruse's paranormal experiences resolved his doubts about God and his vocation. The weeping statues and the stigmata ceased after Father Bruse decided to remain a priest.

The example of Alexandrina da Costa is illustrative. In *Making Saints*, Kenneth L. Woodward notes that at the time of her death in 1955 at the age of fifty-one, Alexandrina was the most famous religious figure in Portugal after the children at Fatima. After an accident when she was twenty left her bedridden, Alexandrina initially had visions of the devil who, she said, tempted her with obscene and lewd sexual acts. From 1938 to 1942, every Friday afternoon beginning at noon and continuing for three and a half hours, she went into an ecstatic trance during which she regained the use of her legs and, falling on her knees, reenacted the stations of the cross. At the end of the reenactment, after the crucifixion, Alexandrina reported that she would receive a blood transfusion from Jesus through a "tube that pours out love" from Jesus' body to hers. She also said that Jesus massaged away the wound of the crucifixion on her breast. The church official in charge of preparing Alexandrina da Costa's case for canonization admitted that she had psychological problems, at least in the beginning, but, he said, "The church does not propose as saints perfect models of normality. Jesus loved the sick." He argued, Woodward reports, that "severe psychological problems can help a person focus on Christ." In the end, the official believed her relationship with Christ effectively cured her. "Alexandrina had a lot of problems, of course, especially, her obsession with the devil. But she kept praying. Eventually, she developed a beautiful relationship with Christ that healed the obsession. Psychologically, she was a sick person who was made whole again."

From a psychological perspective, the subject can move toward greater wholeness in so far as he or she expresses suffering and finds a way to embrace it. Problems are not so much avoided or ignored; they are recast in a form that the subject can not only face but also triumph over. From a theological perspective, God acts in these cases through unconscious natural powers—PK and imaginative visions—to heal the injured psyche. In addition, beyond the personal benefit to the seer alone, God acts to help and heal others through public exposure.

Theories of RSPK, or Why All the Walls Are Not Shaking

At this point it is useful to return to a question raised earlier in connection with poltergeist activity and mental illness: If RSPK occurs in private religious experiences, then why does it manifest in relation to some people and not others? As Richard Broughton remarks in connection with poltergeist outbreaks, "At any given time there are probably hundreds of thousands of young people who have more severe psychological disturbances or who are enduring far greater stress than any of the poltergeist agents who have been studied." Similarly, if emotional conflict alone caused weeping icons and moving statues, then we should expect the walls of every church, synagogue, and mosque to be shaking.

Karl Rahner notes in connection with religious visions that some seers may have a "special propensity" for these kinds of events. They develop a psychic "habit" for producing them. Parapsychologists have developed several theories in an attempt to account for this habit.

Recent advances in neurophysiology and brain research suggest one such theory. In his article appearing in the *European Journal of Parapsychology*, Roll postulates that RSPK activity is due to "eruptions in the nervous system." Symptoms of coping strategies (anxiety, hostility, aggression) may develop as a response to these eruptions. In *The Man Who Mistook His Wife for a Hat*, Oliver Sacks observes that different neurological states affect cognition and perception, and that "temporal-lobe seizures...are often characterised by 'dreamy states.'" Epilepsy manifests itself in a variety of ways depending on how seriously the brain is affected. In a mild form the subject may appear to "space out" periodically. In more obvious forms he or she may exhibit familiar symptoms such as seizures. Finally, the subject may fall into a trance. Seizures frequently bring on visions. Sacks maintains that the elaborate visions of the twelfth-century mystic Hildegard of Bingen were the result of migraine headaches that Hildegard suffered from until her death. "A careful consideration [of her writings and drawings]...leaves no room for doubt concerning their nature: they were indisputably migrainous."

Charles Tart, who is particularly interested in the different states of consciousness involved in ordinary and paranormal experience, holds the view accepted by most psychologists, parapsychologists, clairvoyants, and mystics, that the paranormal experience takes place in an "altered" state of consciousness (ASC). He asserts, however, that whereas the majority of people require training or drugs to achieve an ASC, others have a natural ability to slip spontaneously, even unconsciously, into an ASC. He claims that for these people, the altered state is, in fact, a feature of their normal state of consciousness. Some religious people, he notes, claim their experiences come directly from God, rather than being an unusual but, for them, ordinary way of seeing the world.

From a religious perspective, even a genuine trance state signifies nothing other than the ability of a person to enter into an ASC. The intensity of the experience may even result in physical transformations. Rahner mentions a case in which a girl appeared to radiate light while in a trance, but closer investigation showed, "it was a case of ordinary hallucination." This applies as well to a whole range of physical effects seers have evinced during ecstasies and visions. Some experience bodily rigidity, insensitivity to being touched or pricked with needles, fixed pupils when light and objects are passed before their eyes, and other phenomena. Such effects indicate only that the person is in an ASC. They do not prove, much as proponents of visions would like to believe, that the vision has religious value or is of divine origin.

The strange behavior of the four seers in Garabandal between 1961 and 1965 is cited as evidence of their authenticity. Although repeatedly pinched, pricked with needles, scratched, picked up and dropped, Conchita, the principal seer, did not respond. None of the girls interacted with observers while in a trance, and when moved or pushed they would stay in the position no matter how awkward. While in this state the girls manifested certain psi abilities: They could return objects to their proper owners even when the objects were identical—pebbles in one experiment (psychometry). In another experiment, they found hidden objects (clairvoyance) and returned them (psychometry); they pointed out priests dressed in street clothes (telepathy), and, although separated, all met at exactly the same time at a central point (telepathy). Although some people believe these results prove the divine origin of the visions, they do nothing of the sort. Rather, they show that ASCs are conducive to the manifestation of psi.

From oracles in ancient Greece to mediums in modern New York, the connection between trances and psi is well known and documented. To be sure, events at Garabandal were very dramatic and very public—the girls ran all over town pursued by growing crowds of spectators. Unfortunately, the level of excitement generated by an event does not have a corresponding effect on its authenticity. Rumor as much as substantiated fact can attract a wide and devoted following. Indeed, where excitement over an effect produces more—and more spectacular—effects, we find evidence of another aspect of RSPK focal agent behavior: Until an agent is made aware of his or her role in the events, attention paid to the agent actually encourages him or her to greater performances. This is known as the *observer effect*. Knowing that neither ASCs nor psi powers, nor any combination of the two establishes divine origin, the Church has not officially approved the visions of Garabandal.

Studies show that environment and attitude play important roles in the manifestation of psi. In the 1950s, Kenneth Batcheldor, a British psychologist interested in observable PK, in the *Journal of the Society for Psychical Research* hypothesized that not only was PK a natural human ability, but, significantly, it could be produced by almost anyone, given the right conditions. Batcheldor found that there were two psychological factors that reduced the likelihood of successful PK production. The first, he called *witness inhibition*, which he defined as the "initial reaction of shock or fear that arises when one actually sees a paranormal event." The second factor, *ownership resistance*, "is a tendency to fear that one might be responsible for causing the phenomena oneself." By contrast, he claimed, successful PK production depended on people not merely hoping or wishing an event would occur, "but conditions had to be such that the persons involved felt an almost tangible expectation that a miracle was about to take place."

Since the religious world view is especially open to an expansive view of nature, presupposing a transcendental and multidimensional understanding of reality, and since religion does not close off, but rather witnesses to the possibility of experiencing these dimensions, it is not surprising that psi phenomena flourish in religious experience and that religious belief provides the necessary positive conditions for the release of psi. Not only does religion affirm that such phenomena are possible, but also it creates an environment that accepts, and may even anticipate, extraordinary events. Witness inhibition is reduced insofar as the believer, already sensitized to such events—even prepared by scriptural accounts and the lives of the mystics to expect them—is predisposed to be open and positive toward the experiences. In bad times, especially, people look for events to confirm God's presence in and control of history. It is no surprise that the number of religious visions and miracle claims increases during periods of social crisis.

Ownership resistance is overcome by a religious subject's belief that the phenomena are caused by God or a saint. To be sure, the fact that certain forms of religious practice release psi capacities is precisely what led great mystics like St. John of the Cross and St. Teresa of Avila to be wary of claims of divine causality. However, from a parapsychological perspective, ascribing the phenomena to God is one way for the subject to overcome a fear of them. Similarly, once established, religious apparition sites provide a ready-made environment for breaking through resistance to psi and producing all manner of paranormal phenomena that are not, of themselves, necessarily religiously significant.

Finally, a combination of factors may be at work in producing these phenomena. Psychological conflict, certain neurophysiological abnormalities, and suitable environmental conditions and belief systems—along with perhaps other, as yet undiscovered factors—in various combinations function to release psi in a sensitive subject.

In looking at RSPK we see the significance of parapsychological research for discerning genuine revelations. Not only can psi operate in a religious context, but subject-centered PK can also be used to explain some events that heretofore were thought possible only through divine activity. Poltergeist cases reveal the fundamental complexity of apparitional experiences in general. Now that psi and subject-centered PK research are becoming better known and accepted, religious experiences need to be more closely examined in their light. Parapsychology is a useful tool in investigating visionary claims in much the same way that medical science is called upon to examine seemingly miraculous cures. PK research will be discussed later when its role in healing is examined.

4.
Prophecy and Precognition

In 1991 the communist regime in Russia collapsed. To many people, the event confirmed prophecies given seventy-four years earlier in Fatima, Portugal, when the Virgin Mary appeared to a group of peasant girls. The *Wall Street Journal* asked in a front-page story: "Fatima Fever: Did Mary Prophesy Soviet Goings-On?"

To the extent that the apparitions at Fatima are believed to contain specific predictive material, they hold a preeminent position within twentieth-century Marian apparitions. The attention given to predictions at Fatima has been played out in several other local instances. When she was interviewed in 1995 on *The Phil Donahue Show*, a nationally televised talk show, Maria Rubio of Port Arthur, New Mexico, claimed to have seen an apparition of Jesus who resolved personal issues about her own future. When we look at serial apparitions, we discover that, in addition to affirming the presence of the divine in the world, the visions provide their followers with information about the future. Annie Kirkwood, a Protestant woman from Dallas, Texas, who claims Mary has appeared to her regularly since 1987, devotes three chapters in her book *Mary's Message to the World* to "warnings" and "predictions." On the other side of the country, Nancy Fowler, a seer from Conyers, Georgia, claims Mary appears to her on a monthly basis, bringing both personal and communal messages about the future. In the summer of 2001, Mary Reilly, forty-three, a craft and novelty storeowner in

Skaneateles, New York, claimed to be receiving weekly visits from the Virgin Mary. Unlike the warnings relayed by Kirkwood, Reilly's apparition figure passed along gentle messages urging people to pray the rosary. Not surprisingly, many visitors have sought out private interviews with seers, desiring to discover information about their own futures. The similarity between contemporary religious seers and the classical tradition of oracles is an area that warrants closer examination.

Within the larger social context, there has been a marked and significant increase in the public's interest in the paranormal—especially in the area of knowledge about the future. According to a 1988 National Chamber of Commerce survey, Americans spend more than $35 million a year on astrology readings. Horoscope columns rank behind only crossword puzzles and sports columns as the most widely run features in newspapers, according to the Newspaper Advertising Bureau. A number of cities have horoscope dial-in services for daily updates. Ever since astrologer Joan Quigley helped Nancy Reagan schedule events in her husband's presidency, all manner of powerful and famous people have come clean about their dependency on star signs. Former Treasury Secretary William Simon contributed the foreword to a book by Kathleen Johnson, a Vermont astrologer. He wrote, "I have come to view [astrology] as a fascinating perspective from which to survey...the area of finance and to anticipate trends in the world marketplace." Rosemary Altea, a transplanted English psychic and channeler, counts CEOs, publishers, and fashion designers among her roster of clients who want to speak to dead relatives, get advice in financial and real estates investments, and choose a mate.

Events such as these raise a host of questions: Can religious prophecy be distinguished from foretelling the future? What role, if any, does precognition play in prophecy? Who is a prophet? In what way is prophecy different from prediction? Is prophecy mainly or merely a prediction about future events in a religious context? Further, can the origin of a prophecy be determined by whether or not its predictive element comes to pass?

In order to answer these questions, a working definition of prophecy is needed. At the beginning of the chapter on prophecies in *Visions and Prophecies*, Karl Rahner says that "what we today call prophecy—that is, a prediction or a foresight of a future event which could not be known by ordinary human means—occurs in the most various forms." He goes on to provide a fivefold typology of prophecy, examining its various popular conceptions in order to arrive at a genuine religious understanding of the prophetic future. Prophecies, like the visions through which they are usually communicated, are complex events in which elements from different types may intermingle. The prophet Isaiah in the Hebrew Bible brought a number of different gifts to bear in his predictions. Consider, for example, the possible parapsychological elements in his prediction that the alliance with Egypt would fail (31:3), that Judea would be invaded by Assyria (22:7), that Jerusalem would be spared (37:22–29), and, finally, that Assyria would fall (14:24–26). Although it makes the task of discernment more difficult, nevertheless Rahner asserts, "nothing intelligible can be said of prophecies" until these distinctions are made.

Soothsaying and Divination

Rahner calls "fundamentally irreligious" all forms of soothsaying or divination that "claim to possess a technique for wrestling God's secrets from him" or that seek "magical" knowledge of the future. He cites such practices as astrology, chiromancy, oracular practices, tarot-card reading, necromancy, and so on, "which claim to be able to foretell details which depend on future free decision." In such cases the diviner (astrologer, oracle, or medium) is concerned with predicting specific, discrete, often personal future events. An authentic prophet on the other hand, is concerned with a transcendent vision of the universal future. The diviner wants to know what the future is in order to have control over it. For instance, if I know in advance which horse will win the Kentucky Derby, I can place my bet accordingly. The prophet, by contrast, speaks of what the future will be *in order to transform the present*. Unlike the diviner, the prophet is committed to higher moral principles. The prophet speaks about tomorrow only to bring about moral reform today.

Rahner concludes by saying that "where prophecy is irreligious (in the attitude from which it arises, in the belief that one has a sure technique for prophecy that can always be applied, etc.) and profane (i.e., at the service of worldly ambitions, of financial and similar advantages), then the case is one of divination and must be rejected." In other words, if the "prophet" claims to have a "can't lose" system to make us rich, we can be sure it's not God talking.

Fabricated Prophecies

Rahner also speaks of fabricated prophecies, by which he means those "which in the garb of prophecy put forward ideas on civil or ecclesiastical government and in some cases pronounce judgments on the past (which is presented as still in the future)." These pronouncements generally have a "tendentious

political or religious composition (often profoundly clever),"
and are offered as a means to accomplish a particular objective.
Such prophecies are not necessarily the work of schemers or
charlatans; they may occur even among those who are otherwise
noted for their saintliness. Rahner cites the example of a manuscript "discovered" in 1590 allegedly written by St. Malachy in
1139. In it Malachy records a vision containing a list of the traits
of all future popes. The prevailing view is that the manuscript is
a forgery fabricated by a school of Jesuits in the 1600s. Another
example Rahner refers to is the "prophecies of Lehnin," a one-
hundred verse poem reputedly written by the monk Hermann
of Lehnin around the year 1300, that was "discovered" about
1690. The prophecy details the rise and fall of the ruling
Hohenzolleren dynasty in Germany and the restoration of the
Roman Catholic Church. However the account is only historically correct up to the year 1688; all of the subsequent predictions are false. The poem is believed to be a forgery written
around 1684 by a Lutheran pastor who had trouble with government authorities.

Anticipating the Future

A third type of prophecy "anticipates the future (at least
attempts to do so) in the light of the philosophy and theology
of history." Throughout history, Rahner says, there have been
"great human minds" capable of "frequent and uncannily accurate intuitions of the future." Such people do not so much predict an unknown future as they project onto the future from
their knowledge of the past and their insight into the present.
They do not foretell; rather they forecast what will be—given
what has been and what is already. Hence their prophecies are

"inseparable from their particular historical perspective and limited accordingly."

To the degree that the historical future emerges out of seeds planted in the present, the success of these prophecies depends on the perspicacity of a person deducing which seeds will take root and flower. For example, at the close of World War I an insightful mind, by reading the terms of the Versailles treaty, could have foreseen the coming of World War II already in embryo. "As such prophecies always prove to be deductions from an analysis of the present," Rahner says, "they can be distinguished from supernatural prophecy with relative ease."

Significantly, Rahner points to a well-known truth that anticipating the future can have a self-fulfilling effect. "Many things will happen not because they were foreseen, but because they were 'predicted' of a future 'utopia' which will attract people as a new idea and inspire them to realize it." In such cases, "the future is not foretold because it is going to happen, it happens because it has been foretold." Anticipating the future catalyzes the realization of the envisioned end.

In an article in the *International Journal of Parapsychology*, psychologist Jan Ehrenwald claims that all forms of foretelling the future are essentially "needs based"—that is, the result of a "circular pattern of feedback of emotionally charged needs, wishes and expectations of those persons involved." This pattern has a marked tendency for self-fulfillment and is especially powerful in public prophecies.

As one example, Ehrenwald cites the impact of Isaiah's prophecy that a "remnant will return" (10:21–22) on the Zionist movement, that culminated in the founding of the State of Israel. Ehrenwald calls these types of prophecy "historically effective," in that the predictions serve to influence distant future historical actions.

The self-fulfilling dimension of prophecy has two important consequences for discerning genuine divine communication. First, the predictive success of a prophecy does not guarantee its origin. If the future does not merely happen but comes about, at least in part, by virtue of human cooperation and participation, and if foretelling the future can bring about that which is foretold, then the divine origin of a prophecy is not confirmed solely on the grounds that the prediction came true. Once a prophet speaks, the event predicted is anticipated and can be precipitated by those who hear it. When Isaiah said that Judea would be conquered by Assyria, the words either exposed or caused a weakening in the Judean people's resolve. At the same time it bolstered the Assyrian forces to the extent that the predicted event came to pass: Judea was defeated. In this way the *activity* of prophesying can have a significant effect on future events. One exception would be a situation in which the foretold event is one that only God could bring about. Insofar as the coming to pass of this event could be realized by God alone, then a successful outcome would point directly to God as the source of the revelation. This will be looked at more closely in the discussion of Fatima, below.

Second, the self-fulfilling character of prophecy challenges the conception that prophecy is a kind of knowledge human beings cannot learn by themselves, but is information that God alone possesses. For many people, prophecy flows out of the assumption that God alone knows some things are going to happen. To be sure, God knows many things we do not, including information about future events. It is also possible, in principle, that God might choose to reveal something of them to the world. However, given that prophecy entails communication, and given that prophecy, once communicated (in part for that reason), tends to foster its own fulfillment, it is impossible to know after the fact of the event that only God knew in advance that it was going to happen. Indeed, the only future events of which we can be certain that God alone has prior knowledge are those that God does not reveal. This is the same conclusion reached in chapter 2 in connection with postmortem survival. There we saw that there is no information an apparition figure could provide that could not be obtained from living sources through telepathy or clairvoyance—except what God alone knows. (This, of course, assumes that God's mind is not subject to telepathy.) The same is true of prophecy: The coming to pass of a prediction is no proof of its divine origin. In fact, whatever genuine prophecy is and however it works, the one thing that is clear is that genuine prophecy is not mystical gossip, a heavenly, "Hear it here first," news service.

Precognition

The next type of prophecy involves cases where people correctly predict events whose accuracy is not the result of self-fulfillment, deduction, or divine communication, but the result of natural precognitive abilities. Precognition is knowledge of the future obtained through no known process of the mind or senses. The precise nature of precognition is perhaps one of the most ambiguous topics within parapsychology. Parapsychologists and theologians are disturbed by the possibility and consequences of a future that can be known "ahead of time." However, according to the *Encyclopedia of Mystical and Paranormal Experience*, precognition is the most frequently reported of all psi experiences. If psi can overcome distance, then why not time?

Rahner's view of predictions arising from parapsychological abilities, through telepathy and precognition, is straightforward and succinct. "They do not imply a special intervention of God," he concludes, "because, though extraordinary, they derive from natural faculties...and must be attributed to natural powers." This view—a reaffirmation of the tradition established in the eighteenth century by Benedict XIV—applies even when these powers manifest in mystics, saints, and religious people, notwithstanding that "in them they may serve some religious purpose." Despite St. Teresa's confident assertion that her knowledge of future events came directly from God—"I have plenty of proof concerning those cases when the locutions are of God. I have been told things two or three years beforehand that have afterwards been fulfilled, and so far none of them has proved untrue"—her insights could well be the result of precognitive ability. Similarly, precognition, rather than anticipation of the future or divine inspiration, offers a reasonable alternative explanation for Padre Pio's alleged prediction to Karol Wojtyla in 1947 that Wojtyla would one day be pope and the target of an assassination attempt.

Note, too, how in both of the aforementioned cases the divine origin of the prediction is believed "proven" because the foretold events came true. However, even when an accurate prediction is not the result of an influence from the past or an anticipation of a hoped-for future, supernatural agency is neither established nor justified. What these predictions do establish is that human beings have access to aspects of the future through natural extrasensory channels. It is neither surprising nor unusual that saints and mystics—people who devote their lives to experiencing reality at a level beyond ordinary knowledge—should be prominently numbered in this group.

Genuine Religious Prophecy

There are three principal distinctions between natural precognitive knowledge of the future and prophetic revelation of divine origin. First, the content of the former, Rahner says, lacks "any real religious purpose and integration into a theological interpretation of history." Precognitive "visions" are just that—more or less clear images of an event—and no more. They provide no insight into God's purposes. Prophetic visions are rooted in a God-centered view of history, and their intent is a value-laden commentary on that history. In a revealing passage in her recollections of Fatima, Lucia, the principal seer there, admits that the visions did not contain any theological interpretation.

Second, Rahner says, "the parapsychological vision of the future is just a vision." It provides a "small," "random," "isolated," "impersonal," "shred" of the future. A parapsychological vision manages to capture only a glimpse of the future, "like an incident cut from a long film," taken out of context "without reference to any larger, coherent event, without any interpretation, any accompanying person to impart the revelation and personally address the visionary," claims Rahner. What is seen is what will be, a preview of some future concrete event. Hence, the seer is like "a reporter miraculously transported into the future who then narrates what he experiences on the spot." Insofar as what is experienced is a mere fragment, "all attempts at interpretation remain unintelligible." Premonitions of the coal hill disaster in Aberfan, Wales, serve as a good example. At 9:15 A.M., on October 21, 1966, a coal hill slid down burying a school in coal refuse and killing 128 children and 6 adults. One newspaper described it as "the greatest single disaster that has ever hit our people in peace time." A study of the cases of people who had visions of a disaster and reported or wrote them down beforehand, showed that no one precognition contained sufficient information for the seer to identify the exact location and warn people of the forthcoming tragedy. Moreover, even if someone had seen the whole event in detail, it would still need interpretation in light of questions about the purpose and direction of history. How does the suffocation of 134 people fit in with and advance our understanding of God's purposes in creation? What does the event *mean* for belief in God's providential care? What *sense* does this future make?

By contrast, Rahner explains, "when the Lord of the world and history, transcendent over time, imparts information about the future, this is not a 'vision' (at least essentially) but a 'word.'" Divine prophecy involves communication, not merely representation; interpretation, not narration; integration, not fragmentation; moral direction in the present, not manipulation of the future. It preserves freedom; it does not bind people to a predetermined fate. It builds confidence and hope, not insecurity and despair.

Third, parapsychological visions "occur involuntarily, and therefore the seer can have no moral responsibility for them." The purpose of prophecy, Abraham Heschel says in *The Prophets*, "is to conquer callousness, to change the inner man as well as to revolutionize history." Benedict XIV distinguished natural prophecy—what we today call precognition—from genuine prophecy on the grounds that the former was an instinct not necessarily correlative with moral goodness. In a precognitive vision, the percipient is morally neutral; what was seen is reported. The prophet, on the other hand, Heschel writes, "above all reminds us of the moral state of the people:

Few are guilty but all are responsible." Whereas precognitive visions of the future are like random snapshots of a more or less unavoidable destiny, the prophetic future, intertwined as it is with moral transformation, is conditional, based on human behavior. (In the overwhelming majority of cases people who have had precognitive visions of the future are unable to prevent their coming to pass.) In genuine religious prophecy the future is open, disaster is avoidable through moral conversion. What is essential in a prophetic word but not in a parapsychological vision of the future is precisely this quality of divine moral outrage.

To be sure, Rahner observes, the main difficulty in individual cases is discerning which type of prophecy one is dealing with, especially as elements from different kinds intermingle. For example, there are cases where a religious interpretation is added by the seer based on his or her "other opinions and beliefs," but that is not found in the original vision.

During the Franco-Prussian War in 1871, in the village of Pontmain, France, Eugene Barbadette, age twelve, called his stepfather and brother to look at a female figure suspended in the sky. While staring at the figure, Eugene and three other children saw a series of written messages around the figure including, "God will soon answer your prayers." On the day of the vision the invading German army is only a few miles from Pontmain. At exactly the same time that Eugene first sees the figure, the German general decided to halt the advance. Is it possible that the central, primary event here is precognitive or telepathic knowledge of the German retreat to which Eugene added, albeit unconsciously, the religious elements? Setting paranormal experiences within a religious context effectively overcomes the fear and anxiety—the "ownership resistance"—

that tend to accompany psi manifestations. To be sure, being spared so near and certain an attack would seem like a miracle in response to prayers, and who better than the Queen of Peace to bring the news? While in practice it is difficult to distinguish when a theological context is added later by a seer and when it is given as part of the revelation itself—especially as the seer may be convinced she or he has received a "word" when in fact it was only a vision—nevertheless it is possible to assess the moral character of a prophecy independently of any predictive elements it contains. A genuine divine prophecy is judged by its moral acuity—not by its predictive accuracy.

Fatima: A Prophecy Test Case

Fatima, Portugal, is the site of the preeminent official Christian public revelation of the twentieth century. On May 13, 1917, three children—Lucia Santos, age 10, and her cousins Jacinta, 7, and Francisco Marto, 9—resting in a cove outside of town, claimed to see an apparitional figure that would soon be identified as the Virgin Mary. In five subsequent appearances, Mary reportedly communicated a good deal of material to the children including a vision of hell and three prophecies—the knowledge of which Lucia kept secret for twenty-five years. Two of the secrets were revealed in the 1940s. They included information that there would be a second world war and that communism would spread, but the communist government in the Soviet Union would collapse and that Russia would be converted. The last, much speculated over, third secret—a vision of an attempt to kill a "bishop in white"—was disclosed in 2000. Applying Rahner's typology of prophecy to the range of events at Fatima brings out a number of interesting features about the Fatima prophecies that have not so far been discussed.

Following the October 13, 1917, vision, the children claimed that the apparition told them that World War I would end that very day.* In her 1924 account, Lucia said that she was not paying full attention during this apparition and may have confused the dates. In later accounts, Lucia simply admitted she made a mistake. While it is reasonable to suppose that the first account—taking place as it did on the very day of the apparition—is the most accurate, what concerns us here is not which account is true but the significance of the first account as a test for discerning genuine prophecy. If the war had actually ended on October 13, then it would appear to rule out the possibility of self-fulfillment, simply by virtue of the time factor involved; however, it would not exclude precognition. It is precisely these sorts of predictions involving events near in time that make parapsychological explanation more likely. The incidence of precognition is inversely proportional to the amount of time by which it precedes the event's occurrence. Physicist Gerald Feinberg argues that precognition does not in fact violate the known laws of physics. He claims that precognition is more analogous to memory of things future than to sense perception. This memory is most effective when the time lapse between prediction and occurrence is comparatively short. Even if, as predicted, the shooting had suddenly stopped on October 13, this would not establish the divine origin of the prediction. However, the more we know about psi, the less able we are to specify precisely what sort of an act or event that would be.

*The number of books on Fatima would fill a good-sized library. Here I rely on C. C. Martindale's *The Meaning of Fatima* and William Thomas Walsh's *Our Lady of Fatima* . The advantage of Martindale's book is that it presents the story as it unfolded chronologically, rather than, as is common (in Walsh, for example), mixing earlier and later accounts together. The most revealing account, however, is Lucia's own memoirs, *Fatima in Lucia's Own Words*, 1989.

Lucia's second prediction that Francisco and Jacinta would soon die (Francisco died on April 4, 1919, and Jacinta on February 21, 1920) is easily ascribed to precognition or telepathy. Given the region's spreading influenza epidemic, it might also be reasonable speculation.

Regarding the secrets about the rise and fall of communism in Russia, the coming of another war, and the attempted assassination of a bishop in white, the absence of any timetable for their occurrence means that they qualify as predictions only if the term is used in its loosest sense. In the fullness of time many events (and this may be especially true for political events) that seem impossible at one point in history actually do come to pass. Thus a B-movie actor becomes president of the United States.

Both supporters and detractors of the Fatima visions have made much of the fact that the predictions were kept secret for over two decades. However from the perspective of their *predictive* value, even if Lucia had revealed them in 1917 there is nothing of substance in the revelations that would have been beyond the speculative powers of an intelligent and imaginative person at the time. Indeed, against the background of the political situation in Portugal in 1917—the war with Germany, the rise and success of the socialist party on the national scene (mirrored on the local level by a new communist mayor in Fatima), and the influence of Russian communism on the Portuguese government, especially its strong anti-clericalism (bishops were exiled, priests were attacked)— it would only be prudent to keep anti-communist, pro-church views secret. Looked at through the eyes of a rural, conservative, church-based community, those recent events would lead them to expect worse yet to come. They might reasonably

expect the continued spread of the Russian experiment, leading to more and more violent attacks on clergy, perhaps even
a bishop or pope killed, and inevitably another war. However,
even if Lucia had told the secrets in 1917, they can be understood as either general forecasts based on a deductive analysis
of the existing situation, or reflections of a desire for and
anticipation of a different future, which set a new goal—the
conversion of Russia—to motivate people.

From the perspective of our knowledge of God, Rahner
says, instructions to keep aspects of the visions secret challenges our understanding of God's activity in the world.
Rahner asks "how is it comprehensible that God should *reveal*
certain matters concerning the whole world to a person, in
order that this person should keep them *secret* until after their
fulfillment?" Concerning the need to keep secret the mission
to establish devotion to the Immaculate Heart of Mary (or,
more accurately, the mission to promote it, since the devotion
was already known for over a hundred years), Rahner observes
that this secrecy runs counter to our knowledge of how God
acts. "Even if it be said that the time for secrecy has now run
out," he writes, "we are still faced with *a unique instance of God
giving an order twenty-five years before he wishes it carried out*"
(emphasis added).

If genuine divine prophecy is iconoclastic and morally revolutionary, then, upon careful scrutiny, the revelations at Fatima
are not especially revolutionary. When asked by her parish
priest after the June 13 apparition what the figure had said,
Lucia replied that the apparition wanted people to say the
rosary, be good, and not insult God. Put in the best possible
light, this is more in the nature of a Sunday school sermon than
a blistering moral insight of prophetic analysis. In fact, the

priest told Lucia as much, asking why God would go to such lengths to reveal what was already a regular practice in the parish. Already on May 5, 1917, just *eight days* before the first apparition, Pope Benedict XV publicly called for a renewal of prayer life, and he especially mentioned that prayers be directed "to the great Mother of God...the Mother of Mercy...and Queen of Peace" (Martindale, *The Meaning of Fatima*). Further, on May 13, the very day of the first apparition, the pope dedicated all of the churches in Portugal in honor of Mary. While this may be, as C. C. Martindale notes, "a pleasing coincidence," it does raise some questions about the message.

Moreover, regardless of when Lucia received these messages, the fact that they were not disclosed until the 1940s, when the Second World War had already begun and the spread of Russian-style communism was a *fait accompli*, more or less effectively stops the moral revolution before it has a chance to get started.

The definition of a prophet as a moral revolutionary leads us to question the extent to which children are qualified for the role. The nature of the prophetic calling requires that prophets must have a certain maturity with respect to morality. Traditionally prophets are men and women with adult knowledge. They usually have personal experience of the world, of human relationships, and of sociopolitical forces. Contrary to the popular view, the prophets encountered in scripture were not moral innocents; they had pasts—often dark and troubled pasts. In part, their effectiveness came from their familiarity with sin. People listened to them because they accused the people of what they, too, had once been guilty. Consider Moses' exposure to the plight of the Israelites as slaves in Egypt, and his killing of the Egyptian guard, or

Hosea's troubled and tragic marriage. Jesus, who was himself sinless, nevertheless does not begin his public ministry until he is of adult age. The gospel narratives relate that this period is immediately preceded by a time of temptation and self-reflection. Jesus' teaching is characterized by insight into, sensitivity toward, and compassion for the human condition. These accounts make clear that personal maturity and moral self-scrutiny are essential to the prophetic life.

In this context, Abraham Heschel says in *The Prophets*, prophecy is not a "technical activity" in which the prophet's own consciousness is overwhelmed and replaced by the divine. The prophet is "not a mouthpiece, but a person; not an instrument, but a partner, an associate of God." Prophetic experience, Heschel claims, involves "participation of the person in the act of transmission." In the story of Sodom, it is Abraham who takes the initiative in trying to save the town. Although at first, God offers not to destroy the town if fifty good men can be found, Abraham finally convinces God to reduce the number to ten good men.

Consider, too, Moses' reaction to the building of the golden calf as an example of the kind of maturity required of a prophet. Moses chastises the people, but he understands the fear and anxiety behind their actions. While personally innocent, he nevertheless assumes responsibility for their sins and takes it upon himself to plead with God for forgiveness.

Could a child of ten or nine or seven function as a "counselor" of the divine, pleading the people's case before God, and bringing God's Word to the people? Could a child have "negotiated" with God on behalf of the people of Sodom and Gomorrah, assuming that he or she could have understood the moral issues involved? Although in principle it is possible for anyone—regardless of age, intellectual ability, life experience, or moral development—to have a *private* revelation, *prophetic* revelation requires not only holiness but also moral discernment at a mature level. This is not because children lack the life experience necessary to be a prophet; unfortunately many children are all too familiar with pain, loss, and tragedy. Nor are children unsuitable because they lack the requisite conceptual skills. There are any number of children who are intellectually adept at an early age. Rather, what is as yet underdeveloped in children is the capacity to reflect critically on their experience, to understand it within a larger historical context, and to transform their experience into a universal perspective.

We are not speaking here of the unlikeliness or unsuitability of any particular individual to be a prophet. The selection of prophets is up to God. However, if we follow scripture and the history of theology, we note that God chooses those who were capable of comprehending the enormity of the task before them. That is one reason for the personal turmoil and reluctance that gripped so many of the prophets when they were first approached by God. Jonah goes so far as to attempt physical escape from God's call by boarding a ship for Tarshish. Since none of the children in modern apparitions appear to have been favored in any remarkable way by the divine elevation of their intellectual or moral faculties—a possibility that would make a child's selection more probable—this means that the messengers of God are less morally mature, physically developed, knowledgeable, and functionally capable than many of the people for whom the message is intended. Clearly, any prophet, being human, is subject to limitations as to abilities and level of understanding. However in children these limitations are even more pronounced, leading one to wonder whether any advantage that might be gained by utilizing children would be undermined by the greater loss in maturity and experience.

These concerns are significant if we maintain that God not only wishes to communicate with us, but also to communicate *for some purpose*. If traditional prophecy includes a sophisticated and often blistering analysis of social situations, in children the divine voice is reduced to such commentaries as "be good," "make peace," and "pray." To be sure, God has always wanted these things. However, if postapostolic revelations are meant to reveal the divine word for a concrete period, and are not, in Rahner's words, "mere heavenly refresher courses in public revelation or a Socratic method used by God in order to lead us to knowledge of what in principle could be learnt without his help," then these phrases do not provide insight into our particular situation. They offer insufficient guidance as to what is to be done. Of course some people prefer such revelations precisely for this reason. It is easier to engage in individual and private acts of piety than it is to think about injustice and take action to end it.

The question of child prophets or messengers warrants more extended consideration. Unfortunately it is a neglected area in the study of religious apparitions. Part of the reason for this lies in our cultural view of children as morally pure and emotionally transparent. This rather sentimental view of children is part of a back-and-forth pattern in the history of religious visionary experience. William A. Christian, a sociologist of religion who has written on visionary experiences in *Apparitions in Late Medieval and Renaissance Spain*, notes that, in the fifteenth century, children and men were deemed the most credible visionaries, but that by the nineteenth century, "many churchmen were reluctant to accept children as carriers of messages from God." However, following the French visions at La

Salette and Lourdes, in the in mid-nineteenth century, children were once again approved as messengers. Developments in our understanding of the biological and psychological processes of human growth over the last half of the twentieth century suggest that it is time for the pendulum to swing back.

Everyday experience shows that children are not good messengers; they are not generally entrusted with the transmission of important information. Teachers, knowing that children have not yet developed good memory and retentive skills, send notes to parents to inform them of upcoming events. To ensure that parents are informed of problems, schools routinely mail letters to the homes of parents or require the child to bring a notice back with a parent's signature on it. In the former case, this is because small children have poor memories and may forget the message altogether. This is especially true if there is a time lag between receiving and delivering the message, because children frequently mishear or only partially hear messages. Sometimes the message involves concepts children are too young to understand, which adds to the difficulty of repeating it accurately. Often what is important information to an adult is not necessarily important to a child. Older children and adolescents are generally absorbed with their own immediate concerns and likely to forget or mishear a message that is not directly relevant to them. Moreover, when the message does affect them, the psychic pressure of either disapproval, in the case of unpleasant news, or of excitement, in the case of good news, tends to make adolescents unreliable message bearers. The child psychologist Anna Freud in *Normality and Pathology in Childhood: Assessments of Development* explains that memory regression with respect to pleasurable as well as frightening news is typical in small children and in adolescents.

At Lourdes, one reason why Bernadette was believed was that supporters claimed she had no prior knowledge of the doctrine of the Immaculate Conception. As proof, they noted that she got the message wrong. Bernadette said the apparition identified herself as "the Immaculate Conception," rather than, as is correct, "the Virgin of the Immaculate Conception." Given her age and that she would undoubtedly have been very excited, Bernadette's mishearing or forgetting the first part of the announcement is understandable. However, this begs the question of why the divine would entrust such an important message (indeed the apparition's announcement *is* the revelation) to someone in whom the one essential skill for being a messenger—memory retention—is not yet fully developed. Given the problem of interpreting divine messages where memory is not a factor, why would God complicate matters further by giving a message to someone who, by virtue of his or her level of psychic growth, is not likely to remember it correctly? Rather than confirm the revelation, it would only seem to add unnecessary confusion. We can suppose God might have reasons for giving a message to someone who did not understand it, but what benefit is there to God in choosing someone who can't even deliver it properly? At the very least, we would expect that God would elevate the capacities of the person chosen so that he or she could repeat the message accurately. Are there other figures in scripture or in history whose credibility as messengers rests on getting the message wrong?

Another contributing factor that makes children poor messengers is that they have facile imaginations. Children not only have vivid imaginations, but they also often believe what they imagine is real. Official investigators have long been on guard against this danger. Augustin Poulain, a historian of

Christian mysticism, considers an "overly lively imagination" as the "third cause of absolutely false revelations." He writes that "certain minds *invent* stories and sincerely persuade themselves that the incidents occurred. They are *inventors in good faith.*" Of these people, Poulain says, "we are disposed to believe them, for their tone is one of conviction; and they enter into details with regard to time and locality and the conversations that took place, until we say to ourselves: It is impossible that the foundation of all this should not be true. And yet all is invented." Significantly, he claims, these inventors are otherwise "reasonable and intelligent, although usually in a state of agitation and ebullition." What takes place, according to Poulain, "is a strange confusion between the *imagination*, which constructs a scene, and the *memory*, which affirms it took place. The reason no longer distinguishes between these two very different operations." The conservative theologian Adolphe Tanquerey cautions in *The Spiritual Life* that visionary claims made by people "possessed of vivid imagination together with excessive emotionalism"—two characteristics that Lucia at Fatima ascribes to herself—are to be treated with extra care, "such temperaments being subject to hallucinations." Children like to pretend, and close observation shows that the boundary between imagination and reality is not clearly defined in them. Children often have to be reminded, if not reassured, that the stories they read are just that—stories.

Children also like to imagine themselves as characters in the story. Adolescents as well as small children are prone to dramatization and exaggeration. Dramatization of imagined friends or monsters gives expression to children's fears and anxieties. Especially in times of stress children tend to take refuge in an imaginary world; in some cases the child may unconsciously project his or her imaginary world into three-dimensional space. This imagined reality can be so vivid and "real" as to replace, for varying periods of time, ordinary reality. In "Visual Hallucinoses in Young Children," Dr. Aaron H. Essman refers to this as "adaptive regression," and notes that projection and denial are the two most common forms of regression in childhood.

Lucia's mother at Fatima assumed that Lucia was the source of the visions and accused her of lying. However, according to modern child psychology and the wisdom of the tradition, even if, or *especially* if, the visions are unconscious imaginative projections, they would appear real to Lucia and her cousins. This is because a defense, by its very nature, "operate[s] outside of conscious awareness," says the eminent child psychologist Eda G. Goldstein, and therefore, "the individual cannot try to use a defense deliberately in coping with anxiety-producing situations." This suggests a natural explanation of not only why the children remained steadfast in their refusal to repudiate the apparitions, but also why, in part, people believed them. Since neither Lucia nor her cousins were consciously aware of their role in producing the apparitions, they could claim with all sincere conviction, as Lucia did, that the only lie would be to say that they never happened. The apparitions were, for them, real projections, and as such the children were sure of their truth. Goldstein explains that since defensive coping mechanisms, like projection, serve a protective function, it is not always beneficial to attempt to challenge them. She points out that in cases where ego development is weak, as in children, "the anxiety aroused by the efforts to confront or modify defenses may lead to their rigidification or to more explosive, withdrawn or bizarre behavior." If the initial apparition was a defensive projection (for the primary seer, Lucia, it would be a defense against the friction in her parents' marriage, the ruinous effect of her father's drinking and gambling, the threat of her only brother's army induction, and her anxiety over being sent out to work herding sheep), then the efforts to get the children to recant would lead to the exact opposite result. Challenges would produce more visions and objections only harden their resolve. The tradition holds, Poulain says, that in cases of imaginative illusions, "the [spiritual] director will always find that his advice has little effect," and "this will be a first means of unmasking the illusion."

With respect to the community, because the visions occurred at a time of conflict when people traditionally look for divine signs, many were predisposed to believe in them. The visions provided a coping mechanism and a potential political rallying point for the community as a whole. The children's refusal to back down, especially after it became known that they had been detained and threatened by largely antireligious government authorities, only served to sway public opinion in favor of the apparitions.

Finally, if children are recipients of divine revelations, and if, as reported, three children at Fatima in the spring of 1917 received them, then some of the effects are difficult to understand. In Lucia's memoirs she describes at some length how she and her cousins attempted to follow, so far as they understood them, Mary's instructions to perform penance for sinners. They gave away their lunches and ate bitter acorns off trees. They refrained from taking water, despite the hot summer sun, and frequently beat themselves around the legs with nettles. "Look, this hurts!" Lucia tells her cousins tying a piece of knotted rope around her own waist. The ropes caused them considerable pain. Benedict XIV observed that "excessive abstinences, fasts and vigils...enfeebles the muscular system and the faculties" and, one might add, may be the cause of hallucinations.

We need to ask what divine purpose is served by having three young children believe that the burden of redeeming sinners is contingent upon them. That the children believed it is made clear in the first apparition of the angel in 1916, where Lucia reported that they were told, "you will bring peace down on your country." It is reinforced by the fact that the children did not share this information with others, who, if they had known, might have participated. Not only do the children not understand all of the sins for which they are making sacrifices, but also the sacrifices themselves are of some concern. Francisco and Jacinta continued to mortify themselves with ropes, Lucia writes, even when they were weak from influenza. During Jacinta's final illness she refused to drink milk because she did not like it, only to be persuaded by Lucia that she could offer the drinking of the milk to God for sinners. On his deathbed, Francisco was continuously tormented by the notion that he would go to hell. As a result he agonized over his sins, which included, but did not exceed, disobeying his mother on occasion, stealing a penny, and playing a joke on a friend. According to Lucia he even thought that "maybe it is because of these sins that I committed that Our Lord is so sad!"

Are the offenses of sinners mitigated by these acts? Martindale claims that Francisco's obsession with going to hell led to a "moral transformation" in Francisco, and this transformation is grounds for the authenticity of the apparitions. Even if we accept that Francisco's sins were severe enough to require moral transformation, it is not altogether clear that Francisco experienced much peace or tranquility.

Perhaps the sufferings of these young children were meant to inspire adults. Unfortunately the children told no one about their mortifications and sacrifices, since according to Lucia, they were forbidden to mention them. It is not clear where the idea of keeping some things secret originated. In Lucia's *Second Memoir* the decision seems to be hers: "You're the one who doesn't want to say anything," Jacinta says to her. Lucia's reason here is interesting. "Of course I don't want to say anything. Why, they'll start asking us what sort of mortifications we are practicing! And that would be the last straw!" What does she mean by this? She doesn't explain. Presumably their mortifications were for the conversion of sinners and to bring the war to an end.

In the *Third Memoir*, Lucia says that God "ordered" her to keep silent. However, in the very next paragraph she writes that she kept quiet "in order to escape from the innumerable questions that they would have asked me about such a matter…" Earlier in the *Third Memoir* Jacinta asks Lucia why she didn't tell Mary to show the vision of hell to the people. Lucia's response: "I forgot." In the *Fourth Memoir*, Lucia says that Francisco shared "my opinion" that the matter should be kept secret. Later she writes, "my secret is for myself." She recalled that after the May and June apparitions, "Our Lady did not tell us to keep it a secret, but we felt moved by God to do so." It was during the July 13 vision that the children apparently received the three prophecies, but in her account of this event, Lucia does not say that either God or Mary wished the children to remain silent. In light of this, perhaps Lucia should have been taken seriously when she said it was not God's intention to present her to the world as a prophet.

Conclusion and Words of Caution

The typology of prophecy suggests that what most people desire is guaranteed information about the future, giving them control over it. It would make God the ultimate, infallible astrologer. This popular attitude, however, fails to acknowledge parapsychological explanations of prophetic phenomena. Precognition, where it occurs, is at once an extraordinary and natural capacity. The existence of precognition means that it is not possible to say that a particular prediction is from God. This is true even of predictions made in connection with genuine prophecy. Since we do not know the limits of nature in this area, the following principle applies: anything concrete that can be known about the historical future can, in principle, be known precognitively.

The possibility of alternative explanations once again reveals the need for the authority of the tradition in discernment. The tradition not only preserves the criteria for assessing revelations, but also the means to make the public more familiar with them. To be sure, our insecurities and uncertainties about the future, particularly in difficult times, may make us less willing to ask probing questions about the circumstances surrounding a revelation or the personalities of seers, but there is no substitute for the kind of inquiry upon which mystical theology insists, especially in cases involving children. Such an inquiry is necessary not merely to protect the community, but also, as the great mystics themselves indicate, because caution is essential to protect the seer.

The need for caution is highlighted by the startling fact that the most popular Marian visions of the last two hundred years—La Salette, Lourdes, Pontmain, Fatima, Beauraing, Banneux, Garabandal, and Medjugorje—involved children.

They ranged in age from 7–18 years old at the onset of the apparitions with the average age being 9 years old. The children at Fatima were the youngest. If we accept the angel visions of 1916 as the first apparitions, Lucia was 9 at the time, Francisco 8, and Jacinta only 6 years old. Further, each apparitional event involved some kind of message—usually a warning and/or devotional instruction—that the apparition gave to the children for the community. In cases of serial apparitions, the children also carried messages (mainly for divine intercession) from members of the community to the apparition. The majority of modern Marian apparitions in the last century follow this message-bearing pattern.

It is the addition of messages that turns what are otherwise personal, paranormal experiences into public divine revelations. Take away the messages and what is left are reports of strange anomalous lights some of which include a human face or figure. (See chart 2 in the appendix for a summary of the phenomena.) This prompts one to wonder whether the religious elements, including the messages, may have been added on to essentially parapsychological events. In every one of the above visions it is the community, not the seers, that makes the initial identification of the phenomenon as an apparition of the Virgin Mary. In serial visions, the figure only confirms an identity the community has already asserted. This is also true at La Salette, a single apparitional event that serves as the prototype for Lourdes and later visions. At La Salette the apparitional figure speaks but does not identify herself to Melanie and Maximin who, until set straight by the community, believe they have seen an apparition of a widow assaulted by her son (a "crisis apparition" perhaps). Here the community takes charge of the event, naming the woman as the Virgin Mary and interpreting her words in light of that identification. Following La Salette, people expected "Mary" to bring news and issue commands, and there was intense pressure on seers to deliver messages. In every case, people constantly asked the children, "What did Our Lady say? What does she want?" In response, some of the messages may have been produced, albeit unconsciously, in order to satisfy community expectation. This view is supported by the fact that in all cases of visions with messages it takes time, frequently several separate experiences, for the message or messages to emerge (i.e., time for the community to formulate the need for the message and for the child seer to absorb and express it). Even the singular vision at Pontmain took hours to develop from Eugene's initial sight of a bright light to the vision of a female figure who the passing schoolmistress identified (although she did not see the apparition) as the Virgin Mary, to the still much later skywritten messages. Pontmain can be described as a serial apparition that takes place all in one evening.

We need not worry that our concerns about child prophets goes against Church teaching. Rahner writes that the church does not "approve or condemn such apparitions or revelations but merely permits Catholics to believe in them…with a purely human faith." Thus a Catholic may in good conscience not believe in a "permitted" revelation "without prejudice to the integrity of his faith."

Moreover, even in a case where there are questions about the origin of a message and where the authenticating event remains ambiguous, it can still be understood as of God. To the extent that interest in prophecy reflects a belief that God communicates love for us and to us, and is not just a desire to take control of the future from God, then we can accept a revelation as genuine even if it does not exceed natural human abilities. This acceptance expresses our faith and hope that God eternal does have and always has had, even in the most perilous circumstances, a firm grip on the reins of history. Since the point of prophecy is to challenge us to shift from an egocentric perspective to a theocentric one, then any event that accomplishes this must have something of the divine in it. Wasn't that precisely what the visions at Fatima did for the anxious, war-weary, government-wary people of Portugal—and Europe—in 1917?

Rahner, who has many questions about Fatima, nevertheless insists that even if all aspects of the visions could be explained in natural terms "this would be far from denying divine origin." That is, if we do not treat Fatima as an oracle-like dispenser of new headlines, but take it as an opportunity to awaken and deepen our understanding of the omnipresence of God, where the knowledge of the transcendent and universal place of God is realized in and through the particular place, then we can understand its claim to being an authentic revelation. As Rahner says, "From the devotional point of view it is immaterial whether the divine causality operates within or beyond the framework of natural law, since the religious man can rightly see, even in events capable of 'natural explanation,' the free graces of God given for his salvation." This of course presumes that the seer and the revelation satisfy the negative and positive criteria for genuine visions. It is to the latter that we now turn.

5.
Criteria for Genuine Visions

One of the strangest features of the attitude toward visions and other mystical phenomena today is the neglect of tradition. Contemporary Christians seem to forget that two thousand years of practice make the church very efficient "ghostbusters," with tested and true criteria for discerning genuine revelations. Augustin Poulain collected and organized centuries' worth of authoritative investigation procedures in his comprehensive volume, *The Graces of Interior Prayer.* The book includes such useful headings as "Illusions to Be Avoided," "Five Causes of Error That May Have Had an Influence upon True Revelations," "Five Causes of Absolutely False Revelations," "Seven Kinds of Inquiries to Be Made Regarding the Person Who Believes Himself to Be Thus Favored," "Nine Points upon Which Information Should Be Obtained," and "Seven Rules for Those Who Believe Themselves to Receive Revelations and Visions."

The concerned believer is not adrift in a sea of visionary claims with no secure means of discernment. Help is available. It is worth our while to take a closer look at the traditional teaching on discernment.

The tradition admits two kinds of criteria, negative and positive, both of which must be satisfied in judging a revelation. One can speak of criteria being negative in the sense that, without them, a vision cannot be considered genuine. There are four kinds of negative criteria, all of which concern the personality and character of the visionary.

Negative Criteria

Personal Piety

The first negative criterion concerns the piety and personal honesty of the seer. These are essential qualities for a genuine seer. For a vision to be considered authentic, however, something more is needed beyond ordinary religious humility. The hallmark of an authentic vision involves positive advances in sanctity for the seer—advances that decisively and permanently alter his or her consciousness. Interesting here is the fact that Melanie, one of the visionaries at La Salette, changed religious orders four times before finally being dismissed from the last community; the other visionary, Maximin, capitalized on his fame by participating in a business venture for a liqueur called "Salettine" with a picture of himself on the label.

Physical and Mental Health

The second negative criterion is the requirement that the seer be physically and mentally healthy. Prior to developments in the fields of physiology and psychology, it was assumed that if a person behaved normally and responded rationally according to conventional standards, then the person was healthy. Today we know that appearances can be misleading and that outward conformity is not proof against mental and physical instability. Surprisingly this knowledge has yet to affect the way most people approach religious seers. It is a sad truth of contemporary attitudes that a child applying to private school will undergo more rigorous psychological testing than someone claiming to receive a divine revelation.

Very often a person may suffer from a serious mental illness without being completely dysfunctional. It's not only possible but also quite likely that such a person could pass a standard psychological competency test. The tradition warns against a marked propensity for simulation and self-dramatization, a conscious craving for attention—as much for blame as for praise—and a more or less unconscious habit of deception, as common signs of a disordered personality. These signs are red flags indicating that visions associated with such personalities should be treated with great suspicion.

The practice of religion, as church authorities know, offers ample scope for such personalities. For example there is significant evidence of all of these characteristics in the personality of Margaret Mary Alacoque, a seventeenth-century nun of the Visitation Convent at Paray-le-Monial, France, who had visions of Jesus instructing her to promote devotion to his Sacred Heart. Her life story, according to Henri Ghéon in *Secrets of Saints*, reveals a history of self-dramatization, an obsessive need for attention, intense passions (she carved Jesus' name on her chest with a knife), and a fixation on incurring blame. In one instance Margaret Mary reported that God told her "in the presence of all the sisters she must declare herself chosen by God to make expiation in their stead." It's a good thing that devotion to the Sacred Heart was already known and practiced before she had her visions.

The situation is further complicated by the fact that personality characteristics of this sort are not incompatible with genuine piety. The case of the early-twentieth-century German visionary and stigmatic Theresa Neumann is instructive here. A committee of church and medical authorities examined Neumann on several occasions and found her to have all the signs of a severe personality disorder. However, as Reginald Omez reports, the committee noted that Neumann herself was completely sincere in her religious devotions.

Finally, symptoms of a psychological disorder can manifest themselves in just one particular phenomenon—for example, in a religious vision. In all other life circumstances the person may function by conventional standards. For some people visionary activity may constitute the main channel for the expression of an underlying psychogenic disorder. He or she may be, and usually is, completely unaware of the disorder or its connection to the visions. So the visions and auditions provide an outlet for ideas and emotions the person cannot consciously acknowledge or integrate. Those who experience visions and auditions usually function well within the boundaries of normalcy in other areas of their lives. They hold jobs and care for their families. The visions are at once a means of expressing mental distress and a coping strategy for dealing with it. The stereotypical image of someone who hears voices as hopelessly dysfunctional is far from characteristic in the majority of cases.

The possibility of a psychological disorder coexisting with genuine piety reinforces the need for repeated, in-depth investigation of seers by trained professionals. Once we acknowledge that sanity is no defense against psychological projection, our whole approach to evaluating visions will have to change. It is especially necessary in cases involving children and adolescents, who are generally prone to self-dramatization, simulation, unconscious deception, and attention seeking. Certainly piety and religious devotion in children are not unusual, and do not necessarily indicate the presence of a psychological disorder. However, when the level of piety so far exceeds the usual as to invite remark, and when religious fervor is accompanied by claims of visions, there is reason to be suspicious. Excelling in devotion and having visions are behaviors that are likely to attract a good deal of (much coveted) attention for children.

For example, is it insignificant that Lucia's visionary experience at Fatima began precisely as her family life was disintegrating? Is there a correlation between the onset of the visions, in which she assumed the central role, and the fact that Lucia (the pampered baby of the family), was, at the age of seven, suddenly sent away by her mother from school and family to work on her own? Is it not conceivable that Lucia had already developed a mechanism—the 1916 angel visions—to cope with her feelings of displacement and anger? Should we overlook the fact that Lucia's mother initially insisted that Lucia, a gifted storyteller, was fantasizing? We know how the visions inspired the devotion of her younger cousins who followed Lucia around and looked up to her as their leader and spokesperson. The visions subsequently put her at the center of the attention of thousands. In the absence of an in-depth psychological examination of Lucia and her family these questions can never really be settled.

Personal Integrity

The third negative criterion is personal integrity, which includes the seer's sincerity, straightforwardness, and simplicity of manner. However, as with humility and piety, this test is not decisive. From the perspective of personal integrity, there may be no discernible difference between the manner of a person who has actually had a genuine divine communication and person who truly believes he or she had one, but that can be traced solely to unconscious psychological forces. Where there is no conscious intent to deceive, both may exhibit the same personal qualities. This criterion raises interesting questions about the integrity of the seers at Garabandal, Spain. At one time or another each of the seers there retracted her claims and then, with one exception, retracted her retractions. The retractions are an unavoidable sticking point, even if one is inclined in favor of Garabandal. However, if psi was responsible for some of the effects, then it could explain the confusion. Perhaps paranormal phenomena occurred, but lacking knowledge of psi the seers may have unconsciously added the religious elements. The mixing of these real but separate elements could have led to the back and forth retractions. To deny the events entirely would seem false to the seer, but to affirm everything about them would also seem false. This could also explain why the seer who has maintained her retraction is nevertheless still open to talking about the events.

Parapsychological Powers

The last negative criterion concerns parapsychological phenomena. As already noted, the tradition requires that the existence of psi demands a reevaluation of phenomena previously accepted as supernatural proof of the divine origin of a vision. This criterion is particularly important when a seer claims a vision contains a public message for the community as a whole. It is at this point that the positive criteria for discerning genuine divine visions come into focus.

Positive Criteria

There are two standards of positive criteria, one for the visionary and one for outside observers. These standards correspond to the two different kinds of visions: purely private revelations intended for the personal spiritual growth of the seer and prophetic revelations intended for the community of believers. √

Private Revelations

When a vision is purely a private revelation that serves to deepen the believer's spiritual life, the seer may either accept the vision as an aid to devotion—Rahner adds, "in gratitude and in silence"—or may choose to suspend definitive judgment. In either case, the tradition maintains that the important element is the spiritual transformation of the seer, not the appearance of strange images. This view is especially helpful in the present climate when we are confronted with all manner of alleged private revelations, like the man in New Jersey who believed the Virgin Mary appeared every month in his backyard.

The standard of judgment for outside observers in private visions is the same as it is for the visionary: We are free either to accept the event or to suspend judgment. However, since only the visionary sees the vision, the outsider's certainty must be less secure than that of the seer. Discernment is also complicated by the unavoidable influence of the seer's personality on the imaginative content of the vision. Even genuine revelations contain both human and divine influences. The tradition holds that a vision can be genuine and still have hallucinatory elements. At the same time, affirming the authenticity of a vision does not mean the vision is correct in every aspect and must be accepted as such. Thus, even though the visions of Margaret Mary Alacoque may have been drawn from images found in previously published works, including those of her religious order, they can still be genuine. The authenticity of the visions does not commit us to the belief that they came directly from God. Descriptions of the Virgin that match those found in a local church, for instance, can be accepted as the product of the seer's imagination without jeopardizing the truth of the message in the visions. Similarly, the fact that Mary, in a vision, told

Lucia she must learn how to read not long after Lucia's own mother, Maria, forbade it, may be evidence of willfulness but not of duplicity.

The problem of subjective influences in the content of visions and their consequences for genuine discernment are played out quite clearly in the more-than-decade-long series of visions at Medjugorje. The theology of the revelations is dated, using ideas and language from before the Second Vatican Council. Are we to suppose, as Lucia did in response to questions about doctrinal errors made by her angelic visitor, that Mary does not know any modern theology? Rather, we may conclude that in both cases, the theological sophistication reflects the level of understanding of the seers. The visions at Medjugorje also suggest that Mary is involved in a conflict between the Franciscans and the local bishops over the visions. Undoubtedly this is a preoccupation of the seers. More troubling, however, was a report in the *National Catholic Reporter* in February 1994 that the visions echoed a partisan theme supporting the Croatian side in the war in Yugoslavia. It is hardly credible that the "Queen of Peace," as she is known at Medjugorje, takes sides in wars. If the visions at Medjugorje prove to be authentic, one would not be obliged to accept their political content. The problem in this case may lie in the unusual duration of the visions. In long-term recurring apparitional experiences there is simply greater opportunity for subjective material to invade the visions.

Prophetic Revelations

For private revelations that claim a prophetic mission, the standard of judgment for both the visionary and observers is the same—an unambiguous miracle. Whenever visions make demands on us—demands that are not evident apart from the visions—they must be verified by external criteria that are clear, real, and unproblematic. The event that authenticates a proposition, cannot itself be subject to doubt.

Notwithstanding the miraculous occurrence of the vision itself, miracles of confirmation are a traditional characteristic of religious apparitional experiences. They signify that the message or teaching contained in the vision is from God, and that it has been correctly delivered and interpreted. For example, in 1531 Bishop Zumarraga of Mexico demanded from Juan Diego a concrete sign that the figure that appeared to him on Tepeyac hill was really the Blessed Virgin. In response, she sent a bouquet of roses (a miracle in the middle of December), and her image was imprinted on the inside of Juan Diego's tilma (cloak). It is this image that became famous as the Virgin of Guadeloupe.

In light of the fact that prophetic revelations make demands on those who have not experienced the vision, and given that they touch on grave matters such as God's Will for us, the community is justified in expecting some objective public accreditation of them. We turn now to the historically most frequently cited miracle of confirmation—the healing miracle.

6.
Healings and Miracles

Since sudden healings are the most frequently cited "miracles" put forward to authenticate revelations, they warrant further investigation. What constitutes a healing miracle? The first thing we need to do is define miracle.

The Bureau des Constatations Médicales de Lourdes was established in 1884 to investigate the claims of miraculous cures at the shrine. Despite the huge size of the crowds—on average 20,000 visitors a day—only a very small number of cases have been submitted to the commission for review (e.g., just 995 between 1946 and 1971). In examining cases the commission seeks to know whether a cure is explicable according to known natural laws. Its principal function is to rule out those cases where medical explanation can account for a cure or cases where there is reason to suspend judgment, either because the facts of the case are not clear or because the nature of the cure is ambiguous. So the main guiding principle of the commission is the "principle of exclusion" in which all natural explanations of a particular cure have been ruled out.

Surprisingly, both supporters and critics of healing miracles share the same mind-body model. Both sides presume that mind and body are autonomous systems. Based on this premise, diseases fall into two distinct categories: organic diseases of the body and diseases of the mind including, as a subgroup of the latter, those conditions known to be effected by changes in mental states, such as asthma, multiple sclerosis, certain intestinal and bowel disorders, and some forms of cancer. All agree that for a cure to be a miracle the disease must be organic in nature. However, where the believer maintains that an incurable disease has been "unnaturally" cured and claims a miracle has occurred, the skeptic sees a disease susceptible to emotional influence and says the condition was incorrectly diagnosed. Given that both share the same mind-body model, the debate over healing miracles comes down to an argument over which cases count. Each side accuses the other of selecting only those cases that bolster its own position and of playing fast and loose with the evidence.

Healing Miracles and Psychoneuroimmunology

It is precisely this model that contemporary psychoneuroimmunologists question. *Psychoneuroimmunology* is the term used to designate a new mind-body approach. In *Healing and the Mind*, Bill Moyers presents a series of interviews with scientists and practitioners at the forefront of mind-body research. The discussions reveal the extent to which the dualistic presumptions behind the traditional definition of miracle are suspect. According to David Felten, professor of neurobiology and anatomy at the University of Rochester, the old model in which the immune system—that part of the body responsible for maintaining health and fighting disease—was believed to function independently from all other systems, including and especially the brain, is "down the drain." Psychoneuroimmunology maintains that mind is present in every cell.

This "integrationist" approach holds that all disease is multi-determined; no disease is immune to psychological influence. If he is right, and if the separation of mind and body into autonomous systems can no longer be scientifically maintained, then neither can the presumption that organic diseases are unaffected by psychological states. In her interview with Moyers, Candace Pert gives the example of a person with multiple personalities who manifests different physical symptoms with each personality. One personality is allergic to cats, another not. One personality is diabetic, while twenty minutes later the next personality is perfectly healthy. All the personalities exist in the same body, yet the physical properties change from personality to personality.

While considering phenomenon like "body memory" we become aware that mind and body are deeply connected even when—especially when—we don't consciously know it. In body memory, a person can re-experience a past trauma, both psychologically and physically. The body stores the memory of an injury in such a way that years later the physical symptoms, which can include bleeding and bruising, reappear spontaneously without any external cause. Body memory demonstrates not only the power of the mind to cure, but also the power of the mind to cause injury. From the point of view of mystical experience, body memory may explain some stigmata cases. According to this view, the appearance of stigmata—an imitation in various forms of the crucifixion wounds—is the result of some repressed psychophysical trauma. As with RSPK, the religious context provides a generally safe, accepting, and tradition-backed support system to encourage the release of the repressed injury. Participating in Christ's suffering transforms a dissociating experience of personal trauma into a divinely-ordained sacrifice for the collective good. In both stigmata and body memory cases, a person can feel overwhelmed by capricious, superior, inescapable forces against which he has no recourse. Modern stigmatics report a sense of being grabbed by God, during which the wounds suddenly appear. Their experience is much different from Francis of Assisi, the twelfth-century saint who first manifested the stigmata on retreat on Mount Verne. St. Francis was already advanced in the spiritual life when he sought to be united with Christ's suffering through prayer.

Until recently it was almost impossible to prove the effect of mental states on biological systems. However, as Moyers reports, empirical confirmation is documented in a variety of studies. The first is Candace Pert's research in the 1970s and 1980s that peptides (information bearing compounds of amino acids) are the biochemicals of emotions. Peptides are important because they facilitate communication throughout the body. As information molecules, they direct the body's energies and are responsible for telling the organism what to do at any given time. Since the body can't do everything at once, sometimes peptides direct energy toward digesting food, for example, and at other times may direct energy to send more blood to a particular organ. When we get a fever we need to put more energy into the spleen and less into digesting food. Peptides are what tell us, "don't eat now."

In her 1997 book *Molecules of Emotion*, Pert argues that while we are generally not consciously involved in the decision-making processes of peptides—determining what part of the body gets attention and when—"we do have the possibility of bringing some of these decisions into consciousness, particularly with the help of various types of intentional training." Here Pert mentions the success of visualization techniques in increasing blood flow to a particular part of the body. The rate of blood flow is important in prioritizing the body's finite resources; the greater the flow of blood, the greater the amount of oxygen and nutrients available to remove toxins from cells. As one example, after a doctor told a tennis player that poor blood flow was the reason why his broken elbow was taking so long to heal, the tennis player significantly hastened his recovery by focusing every day for twenty minutes on increasing the flow of blood through the elbow. Visualizations that call on Jesus, Mary, or a saint could be similarly effective in increasing blood flow, with a resulting advance in healing. Further, Pert claims that change can take place even without conscious awareness. Hypnosis, yogic breathing, and touch therapy are just some of the techniques that can bring about change "at a level beneath consciousness." To this list we should add prayer and contemplation as "techniques" that can redirect the body's energies. To illustrate the power of these techniques, Pert cites the following example:

> The famed psychiatrist and hypnotherapist Milton Erickson addressed the subconscious minds of several young women who, although having been subjected to all kinds of hormone injections, remained completely flat-chested. He suggested to them while they were in a deep trance that their breasts would become warm and tingly and would start to grow. Although none of them could remember anything that happened in his office, all grew breasts within two months presumably because Erickson's suggestions caused the blood supply to their breast to increase!

Support for Pert's research comes from Margaret Kemeny's finding that even short-term emotional states have a positive effect on the body's ability to produce natural killer cells. In conversation with Moyers, Kemeny reported that her research found no difference between emotional states when it comes to stimulating immune response. The popular notion that an upbeat attitude has a positive effect in fighting disease and anger and sadness a negative effect is not borne out by the data. Subjects who were clearly anxious, angry, or unhappy had elevated levels of healthy killer cells similar to those in optimistic, happy subjects. This suggests that *it is the experience and expression of emotion, as distinct from any particular emotional state, that affects immune function.* A separate, supporting study showed that people suffering from severe depression—a state marked by the absence or repression of emotion—had a marked decrease in immune system activity. Severe depression is frequently true of patients prior to their decision to journey to religious healing sites like Lourdes.

Altering body chemistry through hypnosis and training the brain to suppress immune response after an immune-suppressant drug is withdrawn have also been demonstrated. Conditioning of this kind reveals that, given the right stimulus, the brain will react exactly as if it were receiving medication. In faith healing this stimulus could create a sense of emotional excitation or peacefulness, whether it is reached through hypnosis or self-hypnosis or by repeated sessions of focused mediation and prayer. Some divine cures may in fact be results of self-directed, prayer-induced changes in body processes.

David Spiegel's groundbreaking study of women with metastasized breast cancer discovered that women who participated in supportive therapy sessions in addition to taking medication and chemotherapy appeared to live longer than women who had chemotherapy and medication but who did not attend therapy sessions. Spiegel's finding is supported by Lydia Temoshek's study (reported by Moyers) of patients with malignant melanoma, a severe form of cancer. She found that those patients who expressed their feelings had more immune activity and thinner lesions than those who did not. Although the precise relation between talk therapy and longevity needs more clinical investigation, it would be significant for our purposes if it only one person's life is extended as a result of talk therapy. Unchallenged, however, is Spiegel's claim that support groups positively affect the quality of life of those who participate in them. Depression, loneliness, and social isolation, he confirmed, correlate with decreased immune system response. The elements of psychosocial therapy prescribed by Spiegel are abundantly present at places like Lourdes. If the support of a handful of people can affect the quality and perhaps the quantity of life, then the healing power of thousands at Lourdes must be at least as good.

Touch and massage therapy, as well as stress-reduction techniques, have been found to play significant roles in alleviating pain and stimulating immune cell activity. If depression, stress, isolation, and lack of physical contact are factors that severely suppress immune system functioning, and, if expressing emotion, group support, and physical contact are key elements in promoting it, then pilgrimage sites like Lourdes are paradigmatic models—and field laboratories—of how this process works.

Relevant to these points are the recent discoveries in two separate studies that the heart and the pancreas can regenerate their own cells. The results "astonished" the medical community, according to a *New York Times* report (January 25, 2002). "Enshrined in textbooks taught in schools and rarely questioned was one truism in medicine: the only organs that can regenerate their cells are the bone marrow, the liver and, maybe, the kidney." All that has changed now. "It was a total surprise—it knocked our socks off," David Nathan said of the results of his pancreas study. Similarly experts in heart disease were "overwhelmed" by the discovery that the heart has the capacity to grow new cells. Researchers agree that the results have "enormous implications" for the body's ability to repair itself.

The implications of these studies for healing miracles are also enormous. For one thing, new cell growth may account for some of the effects observed at Lourdes. If organs can grow new cells, there is no reason to doubt that many "unnatural" organ repair cases alleged at healing shrines were the result of new cell regeneration or some other still-undiscovered process. Clearly cases at healing shrines offer researchers invaluable opportunities to study how regeneration works.

All of the above studies have implications for the definition of a miracle. If we base our definition of a miracle on what is possible through natural processes, then as our knowledge of natural processes changes, what happens to those "miracles" from the past that would not be regarded as miraculous today? Can we deduct them from the tally of authenticated miracles? If today's scientific impossibility is tomorrow's medical truism, then any judgment of miracle is entirely provisional. It was always true that the heart and pancreas were capable of growing new cells—we just didn't know it.

Lourdes: A Case Study

In the city of the sick, it is the healthy that are marginalized. At Lourdes, the sick are both the central players and the primary audience in a drama of unsurpassing grandeur and emotional excitation. They are no longer alone, cut off, and abandoned by society. The city belongs to them. It is their place and their story. Released from the emotional servitude imposed by chronic and prolonged illness, they are finally free to experience and express the truth of their lives, both pleasant and unpleasant. They no longer have to hide their pain and anger lest they cause distress and discomfort to those they depend on. They are free from the stress of being a burden. "It is well known," the poet Rilke wrote, "that the various fatal endings belong to the sicknesses and not to the people; and the sick person has, so to speak, nothing more to do." Going to Lourdes, the sick person has a lot to do.

In *Persuasion and Healing: A Comparative Study of Psychotherapy*, Jerome D. Frank profiles the typical Lourdes pilgrim. His striking account could also fit a subject in one of Kemeny or Spiegel's studies.

> Those who seek help at Lourdes have usually been sick a long time and have failed to respond to medical remedies…most are close to despair. Being chronic invalids, they have had to withdraw from most or all of their community activities and have become burdens to their families. Their activities have been routinized and constricted, their lives bleak and monotonous, and they have nothing to anticipate but further suffering and death.

The decision to go to Lourdes changes all this. It transports the sick person—now a pilgrim—from death-producing despair to life-giving exaltation. The trip becomes the central, all-encompassing motivation of the pilgrim's life. It galvanizes him or her into a whirlwind of travel-related activity. Because planning for the trip involves family, friends, and frequently the wider church community as well, the pilgrim moves from the periphery to the center of group concern. The very fact of the trip—doing something different, going somewhere new—inevitably leads, even in the most reluctant pilgrim, to psychophysical changes. If the expression of strong emotions, including fear and anxiety, positively affects immune system activity as Lydia Temoshek found, whatever healing occurs at Lourdes clearly begins with the very decision to make the pilgrimage.

The excitement is further heightened by the actual journey to Lourdes. Sometimes undertaken in the company of other pilgrims, the trip is punctuated by prayer services and other ceremonies associated with the pilgrimage. For many patients just surviving the journey requires resources they no longer thought they possessed or did not realize they possessed until they were needed. The desire for Lourdes calls forth and expands these forces. Cases abound of people who risked their lives to visit healing shrines. In one instance, a thirty-seven-year-old woman, suffering from liver disease, emphysema, diabetes, epilepsy, and arthritis, made the journey from her home in New Mexico to Medjugorje attached to an oxygen tank. She survived to see herself on the cover of *Life* magazine. There even appears to be a connection between successful healing and the length and difficulty of the journey. The greater the obstacle to reaching Lourdes, the greater the likelihood that the patient will experience a healing. This is referred to as the "Lourdes phenomenon." Indeed, the significance of the planning stage and the journey are underscored by the astonishing fact that no one who lives in or around Lourdes has been "cured" since the first healings in 1858.

According to Jerome Frank, once at Lourdes "the pilgrims' days are filled with religious services and trips to the Grotto. Every afternoon all the pilgrims and invalids present at Lourdes—usually forty or fifty thousand—gather at the esplanade in front of the shrine for the procession that climaxes each day's activities." The emotional power of the procession, evoked below by Ruth Cranston in *The Miracle of Lourdes*, is profound and overwhelming:

> Hymns, prayers—fervent, unceasing. In the Square the sick lined up in two rows….Every few feet, in front of them, kneeling priests with arms outstretched praying earnestly, leading the responses. Nurses and orderlies on their knees too….Ardor mounts as the Blessed Sacrament approaches. Prayers gather intensity….The Bishop leaves the shelter of the canopy, carrying the monstrance. The Sacred Host is raised above each sick one. The great crowd falls to its knees. All arms are outstretched in one vast cry to Heaven. As far as one can see in any direction, people are on their knees, praying, in the form of a cross.

The procession includes two features that psychoneuroimmunologists claim are characteristic of healing: (1) intense emotional experience, and (2) focused or absorbed mentation. As Kemeny told Moyers, we need to remember that "although feelings and thoughts are intangible, the brain is active anytime we feel or think anything…and each change in the brain can lead to a sequence of changes throughout the body that can have an impact on health." The greater the level of emotional awareness, the greater the opportunities for physical change. Proof of this is found in the not well-known fact that the majority of the healings of Lourdes occur during the procession and not at the pool.

Can this impact be sufficient to alter the course of a disease? Traditionally and anecdotally the opposite view—that feelings of hopelessness and despair can lead to illness and even death—is widely believed.

In an account of his concentration camp experiences, the psychiatrist Viktor Frankl describes how those who lost hope in liberation stopped eating, withdrew into themselves, and, soon after, died. Similarly, in cases of spirit possession, Jerome Frank observes that the person's belief that he or she is going to die is sufficient to actually produce the result. Assessing survival factors among American prisoners of war (POWs) in Japan, J. E. Nardini, himself a former POW, assigns psychological threats the same weight as physical ones as causes contributing to a prisoner's death. From the point of view of the integrationist model of mind and body, these threats are not separate factors, but different aspects of a single whole. If giving up on life can lead to our life giving up, then there is every reason to suppose that the reverse is true. Pert, Kemeny, and Spiegel have shown that the old wisdom that "as a man thinketh in his heart, so is he," is not metaphor but biology.

Finally, there is one belief about healing miracles that allegedly sets them apart from all other cures: the belief that recoveries are instantaneous and complete. A close look at the records, however, shows that cures at Lourdes do not differ from their natural counterparts. In the case of Delizia Cirolli, whose bone cancer was officially certified a miracle in 1989, it was four months after her visit to Lourdes that a difference was noticed in her health, and several more weeks before X-rays showed bone healing. Jerome Frank distinguishes between the "consciousness of cure," that may be, but is not always, sudden and that "may be accompanied by immediate improvement in function—those who are paralyzed walk, those who are blind see, and those who have been unable to retain food suddenly regain their appetites"—and the actual repair of tissue, which, "as in ordinary healing...takes hours, days or weeks." Renée Haynes, in her article, "Miraculous and Paranormal Healing," makes the useful recommendation to study the speed at which natural spontaneous remissions take place as a basis for comparison. However, even if some cures at Lourdes are extra speedy, this does not necessarily mean that anything unnatural is happening.

New Perspectives on Healing Miracles

From a theological perspective, the integrationist model of mind and body shifts the discussion of healing miracles away from differentiating between organic and nonorganic diseases. Research in psychoneuroimmunology, including ongoing research into the body's own repair system, reveals how difficult it is to delineate natural explanations in determining the cure of a disease. The presence of emotions as peptides in the immune system and throughout the body, directing the body's energies—telling it what to do—suggests that, in practice, every cure is natural.

In the same way that parapsychological phenomena in the past were regarded as direct acts of God because they did not fit contemporary scientific paradigms, so were psychobiological phenomena that defied known medical and scientific laws treated as miracles. Perversely we seem to think that by crediting God for any event that exceeds known scientific laws we honor God. The opposite may be true: When we define miracles in terms of violations of the laws of nature we hold God hostage to the historical moment—to the limit of human knowledge at a particular time. God is by definition absolute. Nature is intricate, complex, and delicate, and its laws are descriptions of selective parts of a grander, deeper whole. Psychoneuroimmunology reminds us that God is eternally creator, sustainer, preserver; nature and grace are naturally complementary interpenetrating realities. In this view, every cure is divine.

While every cure is divine in religious eyes, the integrationist mind-body model requires a change in the theological approach to faith healing. Instead of talking about miracle cures as interruptions in natural processes, we can now talk about the "science" of faith healing. For the first time there is empirical evidence that what we call faith healing has a psychobiological basis; in scientific terms it produces a real effect. As we shall discuss in more detail below, faith is no less faith when its physiological properties are uncovered. In fact, a faith that has physical properties is a far greater source of wonder and proof of God's providential care than a capricious, arbitrary system of divine interventions.

From the point of view of psychoneuroimmunology, faith healing offers a paradigmatic model of how emotions mediate mind-body communication. Lourdes is a field laboratory for the study of the interplay between psychological states and physiological processes. In particular, the ritual pattern of the pilgrimage—progressively increasing levels of emotional intensity from the planning stage through to the grand procession—provides the conditions for the release of dormant healing powers. A range of physiological changes are generated from the mild experience of "feeling better," to temporary relief from pain, to permanent relief from pain, to tissue rejuvenation, organ repair, wound closing, full remission, and finally, to the radical disappearance of a malignant tumor. In the story of the woman suffering from hemorrhages who is cured upon touching Jesus' cloak, Jesus responds, "Daughter, your faith has made you well" (Mark 5:25–34). This may be literally true. Her faith activated and heightened her body's own defense system. The cure is the result of naturally occurring processes—the effect of emotion-peptides on the immune system—and not special divine intervention. (We will look at a parapsychological explanation of this story later in the chapter.) In *Persuasion and Healing* Jerome Frank uses the cases of three severely ill women to illustrate a crucial element in healing—expectant trust. Consider that if these events had taken place at a healing shrine or had been framed in a religious context, they would surely have been treated as miracles.

> One [woman] had chronic inflammation of the gall bladder with stones, the second had failed to recuperate from a major abdominal operation and was practically a skeleton, and the third was dying of widespread cancer. The physician first permitted a prominent local faith healer to try to cure them by absent treatment without the patients' knowledge. Nothing happened. Then he told the patients about the faith healer, built up their expectations over several days, and finally assured them that he would be treating them from a distance at a certain time the next day. This was a time in which he was sure that the healer did not work. At the suggested time all three patients improved quickly and dramatically. The second was permanently cured. The other two were not, but showed striking temporary responses. The cancer patient, who was severely anemic and whose tissues had become waterlogged, promptly excreted all the accumulated fluid, recovered from her anemia, and regained sufficient strength to go home and resume her household duties. She remained virtually symptom free until her death. The

gall bladder patient lost her symptoms, went home, and had no recurrence for several years. These three patients were greatly helped by a belief that was false—that the faith healer was treating them from a distance—suggesting that "expectant trust" in itself can be a powerful healing force.

Clearly, if expectant trust directed toward another person produces such dramatic results, then expectant trust directed toward an omnipotent, infinitely loving God should do significantly better.

Healing Miracles and Psychic Healing

Psychic healing presumes that people can not only alter their own body chemistries, but they can also effect biological changes in others. The phenomenon of distant or remote mental influence is also referred to as bio-PK: PK with human targets. We want to see what alternative natural explanation contemporary research in psychic healing can offer for some of the effects observed at Lourdes and other healing sites.

What is psychic healing? In *Healing Research* the psychiatrist Daniel J. Benor defines it as "the deliberate influence of a person or persons on another living thing or things (animal or plant) by mechanisms that are beyond those recognized and accepted by conventional medicine." According to Benor's definition, *psychic healing* is an umbrella term for a range of unorthodox healing practices, including focused meditation, visualization, prayer, the laying on of hands, shamanistic healing, and spirit intervention. We shall confine our discussion to the parapsychological dimension of psychic healing.

Parapsychologists are interested in discovering whether psychic healing produces its effect by suggestion or by some more objective means. By investigating all interactions between patient and healer, the researcher studies the effects of PK on biological systems.

As far back as 1872 Sir Francis Galton undertook the first empirical study of the possible healing effects of prayer—a form of distant mental influence that can include psychokinesis. While Galton found that frequently prayed-for people (e.g., public officials, religious leaders) did not live longer than ordinary people, his research was the first to show that prayer was amenable to empirical study and statistical evaluation.

The next major study on prayer did not take place until nearly a century later. In 1965 two British doctors, Joyce and Weldon, reported on a study in which they randomly divided thirty-eight patients into two groups. One group received prayers from a distant prayer group, while the control group did not. Both groups continued to undergo conventional medical treatment. Neither the patients nor their physicians were aware of which group was being prayed for. Patients were assessed at the beginning of the study, then again at eight months, and finally at eighteen months. While the results of the study were encouraging—the prayed-for patients showed greater improvement than the control group—the sample was too small to be statistically significant.

A similar triple-blind study (neither the patients and their families, nor the physicians, nor the prayer group knew that they were participating in a study on prayer) was done in 1969 by P. J. Collipp on eighteen leukemic children. It also produced encouraging results, but, once again, the number of subjects was too small to demonstrate a significant result. However after fifteen months, seven of ten children in the prayed-for group were still alive, compared with two of eight in the control group.

Then in 1988 the *Southern Medical Journal*, a respected, peer-review journal, published the results of the single largest study ever done on prayer. Randolph C. Byrd, a cardiologist in San Francisco, designed a research project that charted the progress of 393 coronary care patients. A total of 192 patients were randomly assigned to prayer groups recruited from outside the hospital and 201 to a control group over a ten-month period. The study was double-blind: neither the patients nor the attending staff knew which group was being prayed for. According to Byrd, "It was found that although the patients were well-matched at entry, the prayer patients showed significantly superior recovery compared with controls." The prayed-for patients were "five times less likely than control patients to require antibiotics and three times less likely to develop pulmonary edema. None of the prayed-for patients required endotracheal intubation, whereas twelve controls required such mechanical ventilatory support." While fewer prayed-for than control patients died, the difference was not considered to be statistically significant. However, the careful design of the study and its results impressed even skeptics. One physician who was swayed by it remarked that "maybe we doctors ought to be writing on our order sheets, 'Pray three times a day.' If it works, it works."*

Since 1988, studies demonstrating the beneficial effects of prayer on conditions ranging from heart disease to infertility

---

*William G. Braud, "Empirical Explorations of Prayer, Distant Healing, and Remote Mental Influence," *Journal of Religion and Psychical Research* 17 (April 1994). Braud's fine review of the history of prayer studies forms the basis of my account.

have been conducted around the world. The results have been so remarkable that even skeptical researchers felt compelled to publish, as the following study illustrates. In a 1998–99 study of 199 women undergoing in vitro fertilization treatments at Cha Hospital in Seoul, South Korea, a Columbia University research team found that women in the prayed-for group were twice as likely to become pregnant as those in the nonprayed-for group. Dr. Robert Lobo and his colleagues "thought long and hard about whether to publish their findings, since they seemed so improbable" (*New York Times*, October 2, 2001). However, in the end the difference between the two rates of pregnancy "proved too significant to ignore. It was not even something that was borderline significant. It was highly significant."

Moving from medicine to parapsychology, William G. Braud, a bio-PK expert, has developed experiments "involving psychokinetic influences upon living systems." Braud believes that distant healing gives researchers a clearer opportunity to study PK.

> Theoretically, there is reason to suspect that biological systems may be unusually susceptible to psychokinetic influence because these systems are quite complex and possess considerable plasticity and potential for change—characteristics which have been hypothesized...as increasing the likelihood of observed PK.

Braud designed an experiment to see whether people "with a relatively strong need to be influenced (calmed)" would show a greater psi effect than those who did not. During prespecified periods, "influencers used visualization and self-regulation techniques to calm themselves, and then imagined the same state in the distant needy person....A significant PK-calming effect occurred for the active (need) persons, but not for the inactive persons. The PK-calming effect was significantly greater for active than for inactive persons."

After fifteen such experiments, totaling 323 sessions with 271 subjects, thirteen of the experiments yielded independently significant results. A "combined assessment of all of the experiments gives odds against chance of better than 43,000-to-one." The inescapable conclusion is that *an individual is indeed able to directly, remotely, and mentally, influence the physiological activity of another person through means other than the visual sensory-motor channels*" [emphasis added].

If prayer and transpersonal imagery can bring about physiological changes even when the subject is unaware that he or she is the target of such an effort, how much greater and more intense will the changes be when the subject is aware? The implications of distant mental influence for healing miracles are enormous. Can some of the healing cures at Lourdes be explained by bio-PK? Before we can answer these questions, we first must examine healing analog studies (bio-PK experiments using nonhuman subjects) and the theories explaining bio-PK.

Healing analog studies are desirable for two reasons. The first concerns the ethical and methodological problems surrounding experiments with human subjects. Praying for one group of patients while withholding healing prayers from equally ill patients in a control group strikes all parties as morally unsatisfactory.

To begin, though Byrd's prayer study on heart patients is hailed as a breakthrough in demonstrating the effect of distant mental influence, it contains a number of serious methodological problems. Praying influencers were instructed to pray daily, but no controls existed to ensure it was done. Further, influencers were told merely to pray but given no instructions as to *how* to pray. Larry Dossey, a physician with a keen interest in the effect of prayer on healing, claims that different prayer strategies produce different results, and an evaluation of the ones used by Byrd's prayer group would have been useful. One study, which did look at prayer strategies, Dossey reports, found paradoxically "that a *nondirected* form of prayer, in which no specific goal or outcome is attached (the 'Thy will be done' attitude), was two to four times more effective than a directed method." All prayer is not equal, it seems. Variables having to do both with the person who does the praying and the prayers themselves must be taken into account. This means that for every miracle claim, the form and manner of praying should be as much a subject of investigation as the cure. The study also answers one part of the puzzle about what makes a successful healer: prayer strategy.

To be sure, the world's religions have long advocated the power of nondirected prayer. Sister Briege McKenna, an internationally known healer from Florida, is adamant on two points. First, she says, she herself does not heal; all healings come from God. And second, God is present in every outcome. When she prays for or with someone, she prays for the person to be given strength enough to accept whatever happens. Even when she prays for a specific result, the ground of her prayer is God's will in all things. To the family of a child with leukemia, Sister Briege says, "I know that Jesus will not disappoint you because he loves you and he loves your little Mary. He will give you the strength you need and he will heal Mary the way that he knows best." According to Sister Briege, people have misconceptions about the purpose of faith healing. In her book *Miracles Do Happen* she explains:

People often act as though you can manipulate God ⭐ into doing what you want him to do. If you believe enough or say the right things or if you have enough ⭐ faith, then God has to work. But through this experi- ⭐ ence God taught me that he doesn't change to suit us. In the process of praying and through prayer we ⭐ change to fit into God's will. ⭐

To the parents of David, a young boy with a brain tumor and only seven months to live, Sister Briege explained the contradiction of petitionary prayer. God's Will, she said, is best and will always come to pass; everyone is "cured" who comes to terms with this. At the same time "our teaching on prayer tells us to keep knocking at the door, keep persisting." People go wrong in prayer when they want one thing but pray for another. "They think that they have to make Jesus feel good by saying nice things to him. You don't have to make Jesus feel good. He knows that it wouldn't be normal for a mother and father to say, 'God, take my child because he is yours.' Jesus will give parents the strength to do that when the time comes."

Sister Briege's confidence in God's omniscience, omnipotence, and omnipresence is complemented by her own gifts at prayer; she is much sought after as a retreat leader. In fact, researchers studying the physical effects of prayer would do well to look at her approach to the activity of prayer. "Prayer is disciplined. It is not haphazard. To some degree it is organized." Her daily prayer schedule includes a three-hour program of scripture reading, and meditation using various focusing techniques (praising God, reciting the rosary), culminating in an interior dialogue with Jesus.

Sister Briege possesses the three qualities parapsychologists and psychoneuroimmunologists claim facilitate healing—

mental concentration, emotional expression, and a unitive, accepting outlook. We do not reduce or devalue Sister Briege's work if we seek to understand its psychophysical properties and processes. Rather, these add a new depth dimension to faith. Faith, as much as healing, is a term whose meaning and limits need reconsideration. Faith is as subtle, nuanced, and complex as the individual who claims it or is claimed by it. Potentially wired into every cell in the body, faith, like cells, operates throughout the whole organism, at different levels, under changing conditions, in innumerable permutations.

Further, the credibility of science is not diminished by the empirical study of faith healing. Healers like Sister Briege offer opportunities for investigating precisely what it is in nondirected prayer that is healing. For example, while leading a retreat in Japan, Sister Briege was asked to hold a healing service for a priest with a gangrenous leg that was scheduled to be amputated immediately following the retreat. The next morning after the service, the priest's leg showed no signs of gangrene. This kind of situation—advance notice, contained environment, small group, a clear problem, and a willing audience—is ideal for study. Discrete observation and testing of both the healer and the healed before, during, and after the prayer service would yield results interesting to religion and science.

Notwithstanding the gains yet to be realized in examining bio-PK among faith healers in the field, using nonhuman subjects and shifting research into the laboratory, away from hospital settings and human subjects, avoids ethical conflicts and tightens methodological controls. Healing analogs use blood cells, yeast, and seeds rather than cancer patients as control groups. Working with nonhuman subjects makes analog studies more efficient, easier to repeat, and thereby more amenable to statistical analysis.

Eliminating suggestion and expectation is the second equally important impetus behind the development of laboratory analogs of healing interactions. If bio-PK can change mice, blood cells, yeast, or barley—targets that are clearly not suggestible— then the effect of bio-PK on humans will be significant to believers and nonbelievers.

Healing analog studies have been carried out for more than forty years. The five studies that follow represent key moments in psychic healing. ✓

- In 1968, Jean Barry published the results of experiments on the effect of distant mental influence on fungus in the *Journal of Parapsychology*. Volunteers serving as "influencers" were stationed approximately 1.5 meters from petri dishes containing cultured fungus, and tried to inhibit their growth by thought alone. Barry found that "out of 39 trials, 33 were successes. This success was consistent to an extrachance [beyond chance] degree."

- Graham and Anita Watkins conducted a study on the influence of PK in awakening anesthetized mice. The Watkins's report called the results "highly significant"; mice targeted by PK awoke 13 percent faster than the control animals. The experiment was repeated a year later by another research team, confirming the Watkins's results.

- In a test done in Iceland by Erlendur Haraldsson, subjects were instructed to try for ten minutes to increase the growth of yeast by PK. The subjects were not allowed to touch the test tubes. Here too, the results indicated a psychokinetic effect of significance exceeding chance.

• In 1984 Carroll Nash did one of the most striking healing analog studies, published in the *Journal of the American Society for Psychical Research*. Nash designed an experiment on the psychokinetic control of bacterial mutation. Tests on PK and mutation are particularly interesting because "mutation is an alteration of the hereditary constitution of a cell that causes a change in its offspring." Consequently, Nash observes, "a PK effect on mutation would have implications in evolution theory. In addition, PK control of bacterial mutation would be of medical significance in the maintenance of health and the treatment of disease." The results of the test indicated that "bacterial mutation was psychokinetically effected."

• William G. Braud's study on the effect of "Distant Mental Influence on the Rate of Hemolysis of Red Blood Cells," not only demonstrated that PK can influence the biological systems of others, but also suggested that a person can use PK to affect his or her own body chemistry. Hemolysis refers to the rate at which red blood cells break down. In the study, thirty-two subjects were asked to protect red blood cells from dissolving when they were placed in ten test tubes filled with a diluting solution. Ten other tubes served as noninfluence controls. Braud found an "independently significant difference between the 'protect' and the 'control' tubes." The odds against chance here are 200,000-to-one. In addition, some of the test tubes contained the subjects' own blood and they were instructed to try and protect their own blood cells. Although neither the experimenter nor the subjects knew whose blood was in a given tube, the results showed "a trend toward stronger hitting in the 'own blood' condition."

The possibility that PK is involved in self-healing is compatible with the integrationist model of the mind-body relationship. Since psi is a human mental capacity, and since mind is in body, then psi will affect a person's own physiological processes. Thus a full examination of an alleged healing miracle should include the possibility of bio-PK acting within the person. Moreover, in some healing cures a combination of psychophysical and parapsychological factors may be called into play.

Along with remote mental influence experiments, studies on the effect of laying on of hands provide useful insights into how faith healing may work. Laying on of hands suggests an alternative natural explanation for the phenomena observed at healing sites, and may work in conjunction with bio-PK. ✓

Laying on of Hands

In what has come to be a seminal study on the phenomenon of laying on of hands, Bernard Grad undertook a series of laboratory experiments with a retired Hungarian military officer, Oskar Estebany. Grad first met Estebany in the 1950s when Estebany showed up at his office claiming that he could achieve cures by a laying on of hands. As reported in his article in the *Journal of the American Society for Psychical Research*, Grad designed two experiments for Estebany. In the first, Estebany was asked to treat sixteen mice wounded by having a piece of skin removed from their backs. The second experiment was designed to test the effect of laying on of hands on plant growth. Grad found that with the wounded mice:

In preliminary experiments the groups that received the laying on of hands healed at a significantly faster rate than either of two other groups, one of which was a control group that received no treatment at all, while the other received as its treatment a warming up by a heating tape to the same degree and at the same rate as that which was produced in Mr. E's group by the warmth of his hands. However, there was no significant difference in wound healing rate between the artificially warmed up mice and the untreated controls.

In the second double-blind experiment, done with barley seeds, the seeds that received a saline solution that Estebany had held in a beaker for fifteen minutes "produced a significantly greater yield of plants than did control seeds receiving the same amount of untreated one percent sodium chloride solution." Grad concludes that the phenomenon of laying on of hands has "at least when done by certain individuals, *objective demonstratable effects which, because it was done on animals and on saline poured over plants, can hardly be explained as being due to the power of suggestion*" [emphasis added].

Experiments done by Glen Rein with the "sensitive" Matthew Manning succeeded in inhibiting the growth of cancer cells in beakers and exerted a psychokinetic effect on blood platelets through the laying on of hands. In planning the experiments, researchers were able to control for a variety of environmental factors; for example, Manning was placed in a room protected from electrical influences. The study concluded that the change "is probably due to some energy transfer process from the healer to the enzyme."

The most widely accepted explanation of psychic healing maintains that it involves some form of energy. In general, parapsychologists agree that the feeling of something going out of them reported by healers is not purely subjective but reflects an objective event—the application or transfer of energy from the healer to the patient. Thus in the story of Jesus and the woman who is cured by touching him, there is an indication that some form of energy flows out of Jesus to the woman. "Immediately aware that power had gone forth from him, Jesus turned about in the crowd and said, 'Who touched my clothes?'" (Mark 5:30).

What kind of energy is it? Hypotheses about the nature of healing energy include low-frequency electromagnetic radiation, morphogenic fields, and biological energy fields. The last of these involves the view that energy fields surround the bodies of living organisms and require proper "balance" to maintain health. This corresponds to Candace Pert's view that certain observed psychophysiological events can be explained only by positing an "extra-energy" realm separate from but interrelated with the mind-body energy realm. In *Healing Research* Daniel Benor notes that postulating an energy field explanation might seem like "substituting one unknown for another." In response he points to the evidence supporting the existence of energy fields, including experiments to measure biological fields. The evidence, he says, is just too strong to ignore.

In his book *Miracles*, parapsychologist D. Scott Rogo suggests that faith healers use a different energy than nonreligious healers. This seems to complicate matters unduly. Unless we suppose a radically dualistic view of the divine-human relation, it is an unnecessary multiplication of energies. Why should there be separate energy realms for religious healing and for nonreligious healing? We suggest that the difference between the two lies not in the process by which the healing takes place, but in the attitude of the participants toward the process.

The hypothesis that some kind of energy transfer is involved in laying on of hands is reinforced by the phenomenon of heat commonly associated with it. Aimee Semple McPherson was the most popular evangelist and faith healer of the 1920s. Dubbed by the press a "divine healer," McPherson regularly drew crowds that exceeded twenty thousand. An average healing service in 1920 would last all day and half the night, with McPherson personally praying over and laying hands on more than six hundred people. Before the service, McPherson would prepare herself by meditation, entering into an altered state of consciousness in which she would visualize "God's blueprint of the human form." During the actual healing service, she perspired heavily, and her hands became so hot they turned red. According to her biographer, Daniel Mark Epstein, McPherson herself described the experience in terms of an electric charge, and those she touched spoke of feeling "a vibration...that was like riding a tractor." McPherson, like Sister Briege, always maintained that it was Jesus who did the healing and was herself troubled by the desire to manipulate God that seemed to be driving the meetings. For a time she stopped the healing portion of the services. As controversy over the nature of the healings grew, people were approached by reporters immediately as they descended the altar, and interviewed about their experiences. The newspapers selected a few of the cases for closer investigation, and visits were paid to the healees in the months after the spontaneous cures. Although not as prominently reported, a significant number were found to be genuine and enduring.

Bernard Grad demonstrated that laying on of hands works on substances where expectation and emotions are not factors.

However, faith healers like McPherson have shown that in some human beings some kind of energy force is activated, or at least intensified by, emotional expression.

Grad himself discovered this in an experiment involving psychiatric patients, published in the *Journal of the Society for Psychical Research*. He found that the mental state of the influencer plays a role in healing, even when what is being treated is salt water. In a sequel to his study on plant growth, Grad chose three subjects: one, J.B., was psychiatrically normal, while R.H. and H.R. were psychiatric patients suffering from clinical depression. All three were asked to hold a sealed bottle of sterile saline solution for thirty minutes. To serve as a control, there was a fourth bottle that was not held. "The results showed that throughout the entire observation period the tallest plants belonged to the group watered by saline handled by the normal person, while the next tallest belonged to R.H., and the shortest belonged to H.R."

What is particularly interesting about this experiment is the part played by attitude. J.B. initially made no claims to psychic abilities; nevertheless, he scored well in preliminary psi tests. His results were as predicted, as were those of H.R., whose level of growth was significantly less than the untreated control group. H.R. showed no interest in the experiment, remaining "anxious, agitated, and depressed" throughout the thirty-minute holding period. He bore out Grad's prediction that depression inhibits bio-PK. It is instructive to recall here Margaret Kemeny's research indicating that emotionally depressed people have correspondingly depressed immune systems.

However what surprised and mystified Grad were R.H.'s results. Although it was anticipated that her results would be similar to that of H.R., in fact, the rate of plant growth was consistently better than the control. In reviewing the experiment,

Grad found that when R.H. was told about the experiment "she immediately responded with an expression of interest and a decided brightening of mood. Also, it was observed that she cradled the bottle in her lap much in the manner of a mother holding a child." It seems that participating in the experiment changed R.H.'s mood from depression to excitement. This, in turn, had a positive effect in stimulating plant growth.

Grad suggests that in psychic healing a positive (i.e., accepting) emotional state is necessary both in the healer and the healee. He notes that it is true even for mice. "Here, significant accelerations of the wound-healing process occurred only in mice that were made calm and accepting by stroking their fur gently for short periods daily." Mice that continued to be nervous even after the gentling treatment were eliminated from the experiment "as preliminary experiments revealed that the wounds of such mice failed to respond to subsequent laying on of hands." So it seems that not only does a positive emotional attitude assist in treatment, but a negative attitude may actually inhibit healing. While this is at odds with Kemeny's finding that the type of emotion has no effect on healing, we can only speculate that venting negative emotions produces a calm, more open attitude that is conducive to healing.

Miracles and Healing Studies

Healing abilities do not appear to be restricted to special "gifted" individuals. According to Grad, in principle, everyone possesses healing abilities. The question is not does genuine healing occur, but rather under what conditions does healing take place? If we assume that some "miracles" are the result of bio PK, then religious experience offers a good place to start looking for them.

Location

Although religious healings occur in many different settings, the fact that a majority takes place at pilgrimage sites indicates that physical location may play a role in activating bio-PK. Since antiquity certain spaces, usually those near water, have been recognized as special and set apart. Giving off energy that both attracts and repels, these sacred spaces became centers of religious worship. Such locations appear to be ideally conducive to healing energies.

The linger effect, the principle under which certain places retain psi energy long after the original psi event has passed—and that may be accessed and replenished at pilgrimage sites by an ongoing stream of psi sensitive visitors—adds weight to the significance of location in releasing bio-PK. If healing is effected by energy, then success or failure will depend on the level of healing energy available at the site at any particular time. A low healing rate indicates a weak field, and as a result there will be fewer psi-sensitive visitors.

Finally, religious healing shrines provide support for the morphogenic field hypothesis that maintains there are realms of stored group consciousness. The concentration of healings at certain locations may mean that whatever causes healing is more easily tapped into at specific places.

Mental Attitude

Faith healing is grounded in a transcendental worldview, an appreciation of reality as mystery—not mystery as a problem to be solved but as a reality unfathomable in depth and breadth. It is the intuition, if not also the self-conscious awareness, that our description of the way things are is precisely that, a description, and not in any reified sense the way things are. This attitude is crucial to producing the psychophysical elements at work in self-healing or remote healing. It includes the emotional expression, the mental focus, the fearlessness that comes from accepting that God's will is being done.

Trusting Relationships

If a positive relationship between the healer and the healee is essential, then the relationship a believer has with Jesus, God, or a saint forges a very strong "doctor-patient" bond. Here the confidence and trust bestowed on God serve as a catalyst to release the patient's own psychic healing abilities and/or the PK abilities of others, who in turn influence the patient.

Visualization Techniques

Parapsychological research indicates that PK effects are facilitated by visualization techniques such as focusing on an image of Jesus or a saint to stimulate the release of bio-PK. Sister Briege advocates the incorporation of imaging into regular prayer practice. Visualization techniques involving religious images have an obvious advantage in reducing ownership resistance. By safely shifting the effect onto an all-powerful and beneficent God, religious healers and healing sites may actually increase the opportunities for and enhance the effect of PK.

Relatedly, in *PSI Research* Daniel Benor theorizes that culturally appropriate images like that of Jesus or a saint are a means of accessing a healing morphogenic field. He posits that cultures produce archetypal symbol patterns that function as access codes for the fields. In so far as a saint is associated with healing, imaging the saint in this role will access healing energies stored in that field. Moreover, the more the image is invoked, the stronger the field becomes.

A good example of the combined effect of mental attitude, trusting relationships, and visualization techniques in activating bio-PK is the case of Amy Wall. In 1993 at the age of one, Amy was diagnosed with permanent nerve deafness. According to an account of her story (*People*, March 27, 2000), Amy's mother, a practicing Catholic who had "more or less accepted" her daughter's deafness, heard about the cure of a boy with bone damage in his ear following prayers to Mother Katharine Drexel, an American nun canonized by Pope John Paul II in October 2000. The mother obtained a prayer card with Mother Katharine's image along with a piece of the saint's clothing, and used both as a focus for regular family prayer meetings. During this time she also immersed herself in the life of Mother Katharine, learning as much as she could about her. According to the family, Amy started to hear within a week of the first prayers to Mother Katharine.

Rituals

Along with visualization techniques, some form of ritual is helpful to summon healing forces. Whether it's the elaborate pageantry of a Lourdes or simply holding a relic to a child's ear in a family service, ritual structure is a part of faith healing. Designed to evoke strong emotions in an atmosphere of intense prayer, rituals may initiate the release of latent bio-PK, either in the patient herself (a form of self-healing) or in the healthy PK-sensitive visitor who, through prayer, projects healing energy to those who need it. In either case the persons involved may be, and usually are, unaware of their role in the healing and regard it as a special act of God.

Group Participation

The Wall case in particular and the pattern of religious healing in general suggest that the number of people involved plays some role in healing. The more people praying, the more likely is the effect. Perhaps this is one reason why nuns who live in community live longer than any other population; they have recourse to a constant, strong, steady group praying on their behalf. Nuns also possess, at least in principle, all of the above conditions to an optimum degree.

Facilitators

While parapsychologists claim that, in theory, everyone has healing abilities, certain individuals have greater awareness of and control over their own powers; they also function to arouse forces of healing in others. Katherine Khulman, Aimee Semple McPherson, and Sister Briege would be three well-known examples. However there is no reason why a list of healing facilitators should be restricted to religious leaders. Constance Wall, Amy's mother, could be such a facilitator, as could anyone who is known for having a "healing touch."

Given the weight of the evidence, is there any point to holding on to the old view of miracle healings based on the separation of mind and body? Once we conclude that miracles are not necessarily physical events that do not interrupt the laws of nature, then what are they and how can we know them? It's time to return to the concept of miracle to formulate a revised definition based on our findings.

Miracles as Special Interventions by God

Karl Rahner's most fully developed discussion of miracles appears in *Foundations of Christian Faith* and is called "Miracles in the Life of Jesus and Their Weight in Fundamental Theology." Rahner maintains that miracles are "signs which ground faith."

They vary in kind, frequency, historical period, and direction. As signs, miracles are manifestations of God's presence to a believer in his or her particular situation. To a person "inwardly open" to the infinite mystery of existence and already centered in the transcendent, any natural event has the potential to function as a sign.

Indeed the notion that a miracle is a special category of God's activity, a suspension of the laws of nature, did not take firm root in people's minds until the late medieval period. Prior to the twelfth century, people followed St. Augustine's principle that miracles were events—possibly natural events—that caused wonder. The emphasis was placed on a psychological understanding of miracles: the wonder they caused in people, rather than on the mechanics of the effects themselves. In the *City of God*, Augustine wrote: "For how can an event be contrary to nature when it happens by the will of God, since the will of the great creator assuredly is the nature of every created thing? A portent therefore does not occur contrary to nature but contrary to what is known of nature."

Following the path of Augustine, Rahner's understanding of miracles is rooted in his view of the mutuality of matter and spirit, the lower and higher dimensions of reality. For Rahner, these dimensions are related in such a way that the higher dimension manifests itself in the lower dimension without altering the lower dimension's fundamental structure (which is already intrinsically open for this expression), and without reducing the higher dimension to the lower. The integrity of both dimensions is maintained.

Because the biological world is not resistant to spirit, the laws of nature do not have to be suspended in a healing. No human being is ever "merely an animal," nor can a "corporeal spirit" be broken down completely into what is only spiritual and what is merely biological. Rahner's view of the relationship between the lower and higher dimensions of reality not only anticipates contemporary scientific ideas on the mind-body dynamic, but, more significantly, provides the existential ground for interpreting them.

What are the ramifications of this view for healing miracles? First, inasmuch as the preeminent characteristic of a miracle is its sign-function for a particular subject, it follows that a healing miracle need not be "equally accessible or meaningful for everyone." A religious person may regard his or her cure as a "miracle," even if it is not so for others.

Second, since the purpose of a miracle is to "call" a person to God in the concreteness of his or her situation, this call—and the response—cannot hinge on demonstrating conclusively that it was an interruption of the laws of nature. This is especially important now that parapsychology, psychoneuroimmunology, and other sciences continue to remodel our description of the laws of nature, rendering the traditional notion of "interruption" obsolete. The characteristic that makes an event genuinely "of God" is not that it contradicts nature, but rather, that it calls into question and radically transforms the meaning of a person's whole existence, and not merely her biological or material existence. According to this view, a cure attributable to bio-PK could still be understood as a "miracle." The healing of Delizia Cirolli's bone cancer (*Life*, December 1999) is a good example. Speaking of the long-term personal effect of the childhood cure—a cure which there is no reason to think was not the result of bio-PK—Delizia says: "By the time it was declared a miracle by the Archbishop of Catania, I was 25. I had had time to think what it meant in peace. Now it's part of my life. People talk to me about it sometimes, and I think about it often. It has helped me live through difficult times: that's what I got from the Blessed Virgin, not just a physical cure but moral strength." Delizia considers the cure a grace of God for her benefit ("My cure can't have been luck"), with the result that she dedicated her life to helping others ("I became a nurse, and every year my husband and I go back to Lourdes to escort the sick"). Thus the cure can be thought of equally well as a natural process and a miracle.

Finally, Karl Rahner's approach to miracles allows for a shift in emphasis from what is or is not biologically or materially possible, to the purpose or meaning of a miracle. It allows us to shift from a concern with the physical, external mechanisms of miracles (*How* did it happen?) to a more nuanced consideration of its moral significance (*Why* did it happen?). By placing the emphases on purpose and meaning rather than on biological processes, we redirect the popular, and to some extent theological, debate on healing miracles. It is no longer a debate over which cases count. The discussion can then focus more properly on the relation between God and the world, particularly on the relation of the believing person and God.

Conclusion:
Some Theological Observations

Using Rahnerian concepts, what can we conclude theologically about "special acts" of God? We might say that special acts like visions and revelations are not really special but are rooted in God's original creating, sustaining, and conserving nature. The experience of closeness to God mediated through apparitional experiences, bleeding statues, prophetic revelations, miracle healings, and other categorical objects are not interruptions in natural processes but constitute a distinct mode of God's self-communication. Although imaginative visions can be distinguished from imageless, nonconceptual experiences of mystical union, they are not entirely separate from them. They are, rather, a possible stage in the development of a Christian life.

In some ways visionary mysticism can be more valuable than imageless mysticism insofar as it makes us explicitly aware of the primordial experience of God. Through these events, Rahner claims, the individual "comes face-to-face with his inner reference to transcendence" in a distinct way. This is true not only for the person having the experience, but for her community as well. The public dimension of much of these phenomena allows for people other than the seer to share in the event. In this way, external physical, mystical phenomena offer potentially wider access to the experience of God's presence than does a purely private mystical state.

Special events serve to reveal God's work in the world, in natural processes, and in the individual's own psychosomatic structure. Physical objectifications of God reveal a God who is not estranged from matter, but is immersed in it. Within the created order, human beings are not "merely biological," nor is nature "merely natural." Matter and spirit are open to one another: This is the *real* miracle. The experience of God reverberates throughout the whole person, transforming the physical as well as the spiritual. Harvey Egan suggests that psychosomatic effects may even be necessary to help a person assimilate and integrate God's self-communication. Moreover, manifestations of God in the objective order are signs of the incarnational dimension of Christian faith. Individual, particular "special acts" point to the overwhelming "special act" in which God became flesh.

The widespread nature of these phenomena reveals a universal human concern with the experience of transcendence, a concern that historically becomes more acute in periods of social crisis. They reveal the seriousness of the human struggle to have something to do in the world with God's own self. The search for God in external physical phenomena reflects at once the experience of God's absence and the reaffirmation of God's presence.

Claims about special events, however, ought to be treated with suspicion when they distract people from tending to the issues of the day or when they offer simplistic solutions to complex social problems. What is true of prophecy, Rahner says, is true of all mystical phenomena: "Prophecy is a mere fragment in comparison to charity, which alone has the strength to embrace even the perpetual darkness of the future, which no prophecy could so illumine as to banish all dangers from it. For love alone can accept such a future from the hands of God as a gift of his wisdom and love." Special events should be distrusted when they lead us to ignore charity or forget the unspectacular love of daily life, or when they put limits on the scope and depth of love—that is, when they are used to buttress the ego-self and block, not open, access to the divine self.

Special events are more likely to be genuine if the love of God experienced in them is expressed in increased charity and love. In this way the mystical experience of God in unusual events does not provide a substitute faith, but renews and refocuses the opportunities for the experience of God's presence in everyday life. William Johnston, author of *The Inner Eye of Love: Mysticism and Religion*, writes that "mysticism is a passage to the ordinary."

Turning to the parapsychological examination of mystical phenomena, the principal outcome of our study is that there are no objective order events that warrant invoking special divine activity, in the sense of intervention from outside.

For any event in the world, Rahner says, "a cause within the world is to be postulated and such an intra-mundane cause may and must be looked for precisely because God (rightly understood) effects everything through second causes." This view also applies to special events. God does not act alongside and apart from second causes. For this reason any theology of mysticism must take psi into account and look to other disciplines in its investigation of the origin of special events. This approach is not reductionist. "To postulate or discover such a cause within the world for an effect localized in space and time does not derogate in any way from the total divine causality, but is, in fact, necessary precisely in order to bring out sharply the absolute unique character of God's operation as compared with any cosmic causality."

Even if, in principle, God could intervene in the world, given what we know and are continuously learning about God's self-communication in nature, it is impossible in practice to establish what God did in any particular event. Under the "principle of economy," which states that where there is more than one explanation for an event, the simpler and more efficient explanation is preferred, none of the events put forward as special acts of God, do, in fact, demand divine intervention to explain them.

This not a question of absolute certainty versus reasonable or probable certainty. Parapsychological research into apparitional experiences, PK, biological-PK, telepathy, and precognition demonstrates that events heretofore held to be possible only by God's activity can be and are caused by natural human powers. Abilities claimed to be possessed only by saints and mystics as testimony of their sanctity are also evinced by ordinary people irrespective of their religious belief and spiritual development. Not only are similar events with essentially similar characteristics found in secular situations throughout the culture, but also, importantly, they are reproducible and repeatable in laboratory settings.

Once we accept this premise, we can seriously explore the points of intersection between mystical and paranormal experience. Joint studies to the mutual benefit of both should be undertaken involving experts from relevant scientific and religious communities. I suggest four areas where interdisciplinary investigation can begin.

The first area is the testing of seers for psi abilities. One of the traditional seven kinds of inquiry for persons who believe they've had a revelation, is whether or not the person has evinced any paranormal powers. Such tests are now more sophisticated and sensitive in measuring psi ability and can be used in conjunction with the physical and psychological examinations that seers undergo.

Second, while some researchers have attempted to measure electromagnetic field levels at apparition sites, clearly there is greater scope for investigation in this area than is currently being undertaken. The failure to do so may be due to the reluctance of those involved to participate, but more effort from both parapsychologists and those in charge of the site is necessary. A joint team could be formed consisting of both church officials familiar with psi, and parapsychologists trained in religion. This kind of inquiry would concern itself with examining all aspects of the apparition site.

Third, there is much more work to be done in examining the apparitional experiences themselves. While some parapsychologists remain divided over the nature of apparitions, a review of parapsychological literature suggests that the difficulty in resolving this issue may spring from researcher bias against spontaneous cases as much as it does from problems with the evidence.

Parapsychologists engaged primarily in laboratory work tend to be less interested in studying apparitional experiences. They maintain that such experiences do not lend themselves to repeatable, controlled experimentation. The researchers also tend to be more pessimistic about the possible discarnate existence of apparition figures than scientists engaged in fieldwork and case studies. The latter argue that improvements in the study of spontaneous cases have produced a solid and reliable database from which significant results can be drawn. Since parapsychologists agree that psi is stronger in actual life situations than in the laboratory, the evidence for apparitional experiences seems more likely to be found in spontaneous cases. Carlos Alvarado argues that renewed investigation of spontaneous cases would provide better descriptive data on psi experiences. It would increase understanding of the relationship between the experiences and the subject's beliefs about them, help in discerning differences in phenomena, and improve the ability to distinguish psi from delusional experiences.

Religious apparitional experiences satisfy a number of research concerns. While they may be spontaneous (i.e., not in a laboratory setting), a number of them are serial. The visions at Medjugorje, for example, continued after more than a decade. Serial religious apparitions tend to occur on a regular schedule; the figure at Fatima announced in advance the date, time, and place of her subsequent appearances. Being steady, stable, and consistent, these field experiences offer excellent conditions for scientific research. For both the theologian and the layperson, the presence of psi researchers at apparition sites or investigating weeping statues would introduce a natural alternative explanation to the usual choices between physical processes or supernatural intervention. This is especially important for those who believe God does not act as a separate secondary cause, yet who may also be convinced the effects are not produced by ordinary sensory means.

Lastly, religious apparition sites generally contain at least one, and frequently more than two, psi effects that can be studied apart from considerations of the authenticity of the vision. Medjugorje for instance has elements of telepathy, PK, apparition figures, anomalous aerial phenomena, and metals changing colors. Real effects may occur even in false visions. Here, too, we may find opportunities to observe psi in repeatable but actual situations.

What finally constitutes a special act of God? The origin of an event or the truth of a revelation is ultimately judged by the spiritual transformation (or lack of it) that results from it and not by examining its form or structure. If special events are events that mediate the relationship of God to the world, then any event can be experienced by a believer as an objectification of God's love and presence. It can be special. The fact that, over time, certain kinds of events seem to facilitate this experience more clearly than others, suggests that some aspects of God's original self-communication in nature are more evocative as signs than others, and also that human nature is so constituted by God as to be open to them. We need to distinguish between God's activity in the world and the human experience of it. What happened to Maria Rubio is proof of this.

In 1978, Maria Rubio, a pious woman from Lake Arthur, New Mexico, announced that the face of Jesus appeared on a tortilla she was cooking. The fact that the effect can be explained by natural processes and at the same time can be seen as a genuine experience of grace for her brings us to the realization that subjective rather than objective analysis is central to deciding on its authenticity.

Even if the image of Jesus was entirely the result of cooking processes, in so far as its effect on Maria transformed her view of reality, bringing her a sense of peace, calm, and happiness that she did not covet but accepted in humility, and prompting her to acts of charity and love, then, according to the tradition, Maria could see this "natural" event as an intervention specially intended by God to be a grace for her salvation. The authenticity of an event can't be judged solely by its physical characteristics; this applies even to easily explicable events. Moreover, the meaning can't be judged in isolation from its total effect on the whole person. Rather, it is the meaning of reality as signified by an event that counts.

To be sure, this view—that it is in the words of William James, the "fruits not the roots" that count in discernment—is not new, but since the temptation to accept or reject revelations based on the quality of their physical phenomena persists, it bears repeating. Whereas many people interpret special events based on a supposed divine intervention from outside, Christians are directed to understand them *within* the context of God's original, all-encompassing, self-communication in grace. In a time once again "flooded" with visions, revelations, and other extraordinary phenomena, Christians need to emphasize questions of meaning, not questions of demonstration. We must ask not how did it happen, but rather what is the significance of the event within the total life of faith.

Appendix

Chart 1
Some Striking Similarities between Seers in Eight Marian Visions

	La Salette, France (1846)	Lourdes, France (1858)	Pontmain, France (1871)	Fatima, Portugal (1917)	Beauraing, France (1932–33)	Banneux, France (1933)	Garabandal, Spain[1] (1961–65)	Medjugorje, Croatia[1] (1981–)
Age of Seers	11–14	14	6–12	7–10	9–15	12	11–12	10–17
Relationship of seers *prior* to apparitional event(s)	seers knew each other	—[2]	brothers/ neighbors	cousins	family members/ friends	—[3]	friends	friends
Evidence of a dominant seer	Melanie	Bernadette	Eugene	Lucia	Albert	Mariette	Conchita	Vicka[4]
Apparitional event usually occurs when seers are together	yes	yes	yes	yes	yes	yes	yes	yes
Socio-economic class background of seers	rural poor	rural poor	rural farmers wartime	rural poor wartime	rural working class	rural working class	rural working class	rural working class
Education/ schooling	illiterate	illiterate	evidence of some school attendance	illiterate	some school	erratic school attendance	some school	school attendance
Religious education	little	failed attempts to learn catechism	some	dominant seer had first communion	attended catechism class	little	little	basic
Prior knowledge of other Marian visions	yes	yes	yes	yes	yes	yes	yes	yes

[1]Apparitions not approved by the Church.
[2]Only one seer.
[3]At initial apparition event, the seer's mother is also reported to have seen a figure.
[4]Ivanka is the first to "see" the figure.

Chart 2
Some Striking Similarities in Apparitional Manifestation, Appearance, and Behavior in Eight Marian Visions

	Le Salette	Lourdes	Pontmain	Fatima	Beauraing	Banneux	Garabandal	Medjugorje
App. figure *initially* identified by seer	no	no	no	no	no	no	no	no
Figure seen in detail at *first* apparition	—¹	no	—¹	no	no	no	no	no
App. figure speaks at *first* event	—¹	no	—²	no	no	no	no	no
Identity of figure suggested by others	yes	yes	yes	yes	yes	yes	yes	yes
Figure identifies itself *after* community	yes	yes	yes	yes	yes	yes	yes	yes
Seers return to place of first event at same time	yes	yes	yes	yes	yes	yes	yes	yes
App. figure seen in light/above ground	yes	yes	yes	yes	yes	yes	yes	yes
Physical appearance of figure fits local culture	yes	yes	yes	yes	yes	yes	yes	yes
Clothing of appearance figure resembles previous Marian visions	yes	yes	yes	yes	yes	yes	yes	yes
Appearance figure	yes	yes	—²	yes	yes	yes	yes	yes

¹Does not apply. There is only one apparitional event.

²Apparition figure does not "speak." The message appears written in the sky.

Chart 3

Some Striking Similarities in Location, Time, and State of Consciousness in Eight Marian Visions

	Location	Location frequented by seers	Time	State of consciousness of seer at onset of event
La Salette	field	yes	Mid-afternoon (after nap)	Hypnopompic
Lourdes	grotto	yes	F¹ - midday S - dawn	F - waking conscious S - altered state (during rosary)
Pontmain	above family home	yes	dusk	waking conscious
Fatima	cove	yes	midday	F - waking conscious S - ASC (during rosary)
Beauraing	near a reproduction of a Lourdes grotto	yes	dusk	F - waking conscious S - ASC (during rosary)
Banneux	garden of home	yes	dusk	F - waking conscious S - ASC (during rosary)
Garabandal	road at end of village	yes	dusk	F - waking conscious S - ASC (during rosary)
Medjugorje	pasture near Mt. Podbrdo	yes	dusk	F - waking conscious S - ASC (during rosary)

¹F = first event; S = subsequent events.

Chart 4

Some Prominent Parapsychological Phenomena Associated with Eight Marian Visions

	Telepathy	Precognition	Psychokinesis/Bio-PK	Dowsing	Anomalous aerial phenomena
La Salette	between seers knowledge of predictions	2 public predictions (revealed)			
Lourdes	knowledge of message ("Immaculate Conception")		healings	discovery of underground spring	
Pontmain	between seers knowledge of German army retreat	knowledge of impending retreat of German army			sky "writing"
Fatima	between seers knowledge of predictions	3 public predictions (2 revealed)			sun "spinning"
Beauraing	between seers	personal secrets (not revealed)			
Banneux	knowledge of message ("Virgin of the Poor")	personal secrets (not revealed)			
Garabandal	between seers between seers and witnesses	personal secrets (not revealed) public predictions (partially revealed)	teleportation of host		
Medjugorje	between seers between seers and witnesses	personal secrets (not revealed) public predictions (partially revealed)	cross "spinning" healings		sky "writing" sun "spinning"

¹F = first event; S = subsequent events.

Glossary

Altered state of consciousness (ASC): Any state of consciousness that can be significantly distinguished from an individual's normal waking consciousness.

Apparition: The experience of a person, animal, or object not physically present and not observable through ordinary sensory channels.

Banneux: A village in Belgium where, beginning on January 15, 1933 (less than two weeks after the last visions at Beauraing), and ending on March 2, a series of eight visions of the "Virgin of the Poor" were reported by twelve-year-old Mariette Beco. The visions took place on the road near her home beside a spring subsequently believed to heal the sick.

Beauraing: A village in Belgium where, in November 1932, five children from two families claimed to have a series of visions (ending on January 3, 1933) of the Virgin, identified as the "Immaculate Conception." The apparition was reported to be holding a golden heart and requesting the construction of a chapel.

Bilocation: The experience of an individual appearing in two distant places at the same time.

Biological psychokinesis (Bio-PK): The claim that the mind can influence biological systems over distance.

Body memory: The body's unconscious ability to store the memory of a physical injury or trauma and to manifest it at a distant time.

Clairvoyance: The experience of perceiving objects, events, or people too far away to see using normal senses.

Corporeal visions: A term used by the mystical tradition, corporeal visions (also known as exterior visions) are apparitional experiences of religious figures believed to be physically present in space and apprehended by ordinary senses.

Crisis apparition: The experience of a recognized apparition figure of a friend or relative appearing at or near the same time that he or she is undergoing a crisis, accident, injury, or death.

Cryptomnesia: The hypothesis that there is unconscious memory of information gained through normal sense channels but forgotten.

Discernment: The traditional term for the process and criteria by which the believer seeks to distinguish the genuine presence and Will of God.

Distant mental influence: The reported ability to communicate with or affect people, animals, objects, and substances from a distance through deliberate mental concentration.

Divination (soothsaying): The various methods, including astrology, tarot-card reading, consulting oracles, casting bones or sticks, used in attempts to portend the future. Considered irreligious insofar as the techniques seek knowledge of God's future to advance private interests.

Dowsing: An alleged method of locating people, animals, objects, and substances (e.g., oil, water, minerals) using a rod, stick, wire, or pendulum.

Experimental apparitions: Apparitional experiences in which a person consciously and deliberately attempts to project an image of oneself to another.

Extrasensory perception (ESP): The reported ability to acquire knowledge and information not gained through ordinary sense channels or through the normal mechanisms for acquiring knowledge.

Fatima: Three separate recurring apparitional events experienced by three children: Lucia Santos and her cousins, Jacinta and Francisco Marto, in Fatima, Portugal, in 1915, 1916, and 1917. The most public of these was the six visions of the Virgin Mary beginning on May 13, 1917. The visions included three secrets or "prophecies": the first concerning war, the second Russia, and the recently revealed third secret pointing to acts of violence against the Church. The last vision on October 13, 1917, ended with reports of an anomalous aerial phenomenon, the sun "spinning" in the sky.

Focal agent: A living subject in whose presence psi is claimed to occur.

Garabandal: A village in Spain where, between 1961 and 1965, four adolescent girls claimed to receive over two thousand visions of the Virgin Mary, identified as "Our Lady of Carmel." The two specific claims made at Garabandal are the alleged spontaneous appearance of the Host on the tongue of the main seer, Conchita, during a trance, and the various messages of warning from Mary reported by the girls.

Hallucination: A perceptual experience of a person, animal, or object not physically present and not observable through ordinary sense channels. Hallucinations differ from apparitional experiences in that the latter usually involve the communication of new and true information, the subject often knows the person or object seen, and more than one person can experience apparition scenes.

Haunting or recurrent apparitions: Traditionally referred to as "ghosts," a recurrent apparition is one that is experienced more than once in the same place to one or more persons. Recurrent apparitions are reportedly listless, unmotivated, and unaware of their surroundings.

Imaginative visions: A term used by the mystical tradition to refer to apparitional experiences of people, places, or objects through the faculty of imaginative projection. Distinguished from hallucinations and delusions in that the latter involve a confusion between physical reality and imaginative representation. In imaginative visions the mystic claims that the apparition is not seen by the eyes of the body but by the "eyes of the soul." Considered to be the product of advanced spiritual practice, imaginative visions are regarded by the tradition as those in which genuine revelations takes place.

Knock: On August 21, 1879, an apparitional experience of the Virgin Mary, St. Joseph, a bishop, and an altar was reported by Mary McLoughlin at dusk on the flat gable end of the village church in Knock, County Mayo, in the west of Ireland. McLoughlin told a friend, Mary Beiene, who also saw the apparition. Fifteen relatives of Mary Beiene also claimed to witness the silent, motionless scene on the church gable. The site is known for its many healings and conversions.

La Salette: A village in France where, in 1846, an eleven-year-old boy and a fourteen-year-old girl were herding sheep on a hill outside town. Awakening from an afternoon nap, around three o'clock, they reported seeing a bright light in the midst of which was a lady holding her head in her hands. They said she spoke of her suffering and warned them of impending famine and a deadly illness that would afflict children under the age of seven. The figure, they reported, then rose in the air and disappeared slowly.

Linger effect: The theory that a psi effect continues at a specific location after the focal agent has left the area.

Lourdes: A village in southern France where from February to July 1848, fourteen-year-old Bernadette Soubirous reported

visions of a figure dressed in white, who she subsequently identified as the Immaculate Conception. The apparition,
Bernadette claimed, asked for a chapel to be built for her. The
visions took place in a grotto outside of Lourdes. A spring discovered by Bernadette at the site is believed to have miraculous
healing powers.

Medjugorje: Beginning on June 24, 1981, and continuing to
the present, six children in Medjugorje, Federal Republic of
Yugoslavia, reported apparitional experiences of Mary identified as "Our Lady of Peace." A range of unusual phenomena is
associated with the visions including: a "dancing sun," metals
changing color, healings, and prophecies.

Meta-analysis: A statistical technique used by research scientists to retrieve, select, and combine results from previous
separate but related studies. Applied to telepathy, PK, and precognition, it yielded results far beyond chance.

Miracle: A sign of God's presence to a believer in his or
her concrete situation that results in a radical transformation of
the believer's understanding of reality and his or her relation to
it. As signs, miracles vary in kind, frequency, historical period,
and direction. According to religious tradition, for a sign to be
a miracle it does not have to contradict nature or be equally
accessible to all. A genuine miracle is one that calls into question a believer's whole existence and permanently alters it in
the direction of God.

Mysticism: The experience of being fully present to and
centered in divine reality and the systematic exposition of it.
Unitive mysticism is the intense experience of God, which cul-
minates in an experience of oneness or union with God.
Visionary mysticism refers to visions and revelations believed to
come from God that appear to persons who follow a spiritual

practice as well as to those who do not. Visionary mysticism does not have union with God as its goal.

Object focusing: A feature of RSPK in which the disturbances are said to concentrate around objects or areas significant to the focal agent.

Observer effect: A feature of RSPK focal agent behavior in which attention paid to the agent is held to increase the activity.

Ownership resistance: The fear of being the cause of a paranormal event.

Paranormal: Experiences or processes that are alleged to occur outside the norms of conventional science.

Parapsychology: The open and critical investigation of experiences that appear to be outside the known laws and paradigms of science.

Peptides: Any of various natural or synthetic compounds containing two or more amino acids linked by the carboxyl group of one amino acid to the amino group of another. Peptides form the constituent parts of protein. The biochemical link between mind and body, peptides are responsible for carrying information throughout the organism.

Poltergeist: A word literally meaning "noisy spirit," involving disruptive effects such as loud noises, movement of objects, and mysterious flooding. Historically considered to be the product of agitated spirits of the dead, modern researchers claim that these effects appear to be caused by living agents who unconsciously produce them through PK (*see also* RSPK).

Poltergeist outbreak: The phrase used to distinguish living agent experiences from those of unknown cause.

Pontmain: A village in France where, beginning at dusk on January 17, 1871, during the Franco-Prussian war, twelve-year-old Eugene Barbadette, later joined by his ten-year-old brother

Joseph, reported in the sky over his house a beautiful woman. As the evening wore on, three lines appeared under her feet: "But pray, my children," "God will soon answer your prayers," and "My son allows himself to be moved." The community interpreted the second line to refer to the approaching German army. The German army did retreat from the region of Pontmain on that day.

Postmortem apparition: The experience of an apparition of a person known to be dead at least twelve hours.

Precognition: The claim to direct knowledge of the future.

Private revelations: Religious visions intended for the benefit of the individual alone.

Prophecy: In religious tradition prophecy is essentially a moral indictment of the present, using future imagery as a means of connecting to the historical situation. Its goal is the moral conversion of people. The prophetic future is open; disaster is avoidable based on the people's response to the call for moral transformation. The truth of a prophecy is judged by the depth of its analysis of the human condition.

Psi: The twenty-third letter of the Greek alphabet used as an umbrella term for ESP and PK.

Psychic healing: The reported treatment of illness outside the norms and practices of conventional medicine. Specifically, the term refers to the mental influence of one or more person(s) on the biological system of another.

Psychokinesis (PK): The claim that the mind can influence matter over distance. Macro-PK involves effects visible to the naked eye. Micro-PK refers to small effects invisible to the naked eye that require statistical evaluation.

Psychometry: A paranormal process in which knowledge of people, places, and events is reportedly obtained by holding objects connected with them.

Psychoneuroimmunology: The study of the relationship between the central nervous system, psychosocial factors, and the immune system in mind/body connections.

Public revelations: Religious visions containing messages, instructions, or requests for the community of believers.

Recurrent spontaneous psychokinesis (RSPK): The hypothesis that patterns of sudden, inexplicable, physical events center on a particular individual who is, unconsciously, the cause of the events (*see also* poltergeist).

Sensitive: An individual who is reported to manifest psi ability, including one who does so unconsciously.

Special acts of God: Those events in which God is believed to act differently from God's ongoing creating, sustaining, and conserving activity in the world. These events generally exceed all conventional human capacities and are, for that reason, thought to be directly and immediately from God.

Stigmata: The spontaneous manifestation of the wounds of the crucified Jesus. The first known case of stigmata was to the twelfth-century mystic Francis of Assisi.

Super-ESP or *super-psi:* The hypothesis that psychic functioning is more extensive than it appears in laboratory investigations. The view maintains that any information learned in apparitional experiences is the result of ESP from the living, thereby rejecting any idea of postmortem survival.

Survival hypothesis: A theory that holds that some recognizable aspect of a human being continues after death.

Telepathic dramatization: A theory of apparitional experience that asserts that apparitional figures are dramatizations of telepathic contact with another person, living or dead. Information is transmitted telepathically to the experiencer's unconscious, which represents the information to the conscious mind through images.

Telepathy: Experiences of direct mind-to-mind communication between individuals in which all other means of communication have been excluded.

Vision: An apparitional experience involving divine figures or associated with a religious context.

Witness inhibition: The shock and fear produced in someone who believes he or she has experienced a paranormal event.

Bibliography

Alston, William P. *Perceiving God.* Ithaca, N.Y.: Cornell University Press, 1991.

Alvarado, Carlos. "Exploring the Features of Spontaneous Psychic Experience." *European Journal of Parapsychology* 12 (1996): 61–74.

Atkinson, Rita L., Richard C. Atkinson, Edward E. Smith, and Daryl J. Bem. *Introduction to Psychology,* tenth edition. San Diego: Harcourt Brace Jovanovich, 1990.

Augustine, St. *City of God.* Translated by H. Bettenson. London: Penguin, 1972.

Barker, John C. "Premonitions of the Aberfan Disaster." *Journal of the Society for Psychical Research* 44 (1967): 169–81.

Barnes, Michael. "Demythologization in the Theology of Karl Rahner." *Theological Studies* 55 (1994): 24–45.

Barry, Jean. "General and Comparative Study of the Psychokinetic Effect on a Fungus Culture." *Journal of Parapsychology* 32 (1968): 237–43.

Batcheldor, Kenneth. "Contributions to the Theory of PK Induction from Sitter-Group Work." *Journal of the American Society for Psychical Research* 78 (1984): 105–22.

———. "Report on a Case of Table Levitation and Associated Phenomena." *Journal of the Society for Psychical Research* 43 (1966): 339–56.

Beloff, John. *Parapsychology: A Concise History.* London: Athalone Press, 1993.

Bem, D. J., and Charles Honorton. "Does Psi Exist? Replicable Evidence for an Anomalous Process of Information Transfer." *Psychological Bulletin* 115 (1994): 4–18.

Bem, D. J., John Palmer, and Richard Broughton. "Updating the Ganzfeld Database: A Victim of Its Own Success?" *Journal of Parapsychology* 65 (2001): 207–18.

Benor, Daniel J. "Believe It and You'll Be It: Visualization in Psychic Healing." *PSI Research* 4 (March 1985): 21–56.

———. *Healing Research*. Oxford: Helex Editions Ltd., 1992.

———. "Research in Psychic Healing." In *Current Trends in PSI Research*, edited by Betty Shapin and Lisette Coty, 96–119. New York: Parapsychology Foundation, Inc., 1984.

Bergant, Dianne. "Prophecy." In *The New Dictionary of Theology*, edited by J. Komonchak, M. Collins, and D. Lane, 808–811. Collegeville, Minn.: The Liturgical Press, 1987.

Berman, S. Hugo. "Salomon Maimon and the Beginnings of Scientific Parapsychology." *International Journal of Parapsychology* 8 (1966): 165–80.

Berry, Thomas E. "Seances for the Tsar: Spiritualism in Tsarist Society and Literature." Part III. *Journal of Religion and Psychical Research* 7 (1984): 5–16.

Blenkinsopp, Joseph. *A History of Prophecy in Israel*. Philadelphia: Westminster Press, 1983.

Braud, William G. "Distant Mental Influence of Rate of Hemolysis of Human Red Blood Cells." *Journal of the American Society for Psychical Research* 84 (1990): 1–24.

———. "Empirical Explorations of Prayer, Distant Healing, and Remote Mental Influence." *Journal of Religion and Psychical Research* 17 (April 1994): 62–73.

Braud, William, and Marilyn Schlitz. "Psychokinetic Influence on Electrodermal Activity." *Journal of Parapsychology* 47 (1983): 95–119.

Broughton, Richard. *Parapsychology.* New York: Ballantine Books, 1991.

Brown, Peter. *The Cult of the Saints.* Chicago: The University of Chicago Press, 1987.

Buzby, Dallas. "Precognition and Psychological Variables." *Journal of Parapsychology* 32 (1968): 39–46.

Byrd, Randolph C. "Positive Therapeutic Effects of Intercessory Prayer in a Coronary Care Unit Population." *Southern Medical Journal* 81:7 (1988): 826–29.

Calof, David. "Facing the Truth about False Memory." *Networker* (September-October 1993): 39–45.

Callahan, Annice. "The Visions of Margaret Mary Alacoque from a Rahnerian Perspective." In *Modern Christian Spirituality,* edited by Bradley C. Hanson. 183–200. Atlanta: Scholars Press, 1990.

Carroll, Michael. *The Cult of the Virgin Mary.* Princeton, N.J.: Princeton University Press, 1986.

Carse, James. *Breakfast at the Victory: The Mysticism of Ordinary Experience.* San Francisco: Harper & Row, 1994.

Christian, William A. *Apparitions in Late Medieval and Renaissance Spain.* Princeton, N.J.: Princeton University Press, 1981.

———. *Moving Crucifixes in Modern Spain.* Princeton, N.J.: Princeton University Press, 1992.

———. *Visionaries: The Spanish Republic in the Reign of Christ.* Berkeley: University of California Press, 1996.

Collins, John E. *Mysticism and New Paradigm Psychology.* Savage, Md.: Rowman and Littlefield Publishers, 1991.

Collipp, P. J. "The Efficacy of Prayer: A Triple Blind Study." *Medical Times* 97, no. 5 (1969): 201–4.

Cranston, Ruth. *The Miracle of Lourdes.* New York: Doubleday, 1955.

Cunningham, Lawrence. "A Decade of Research on the Saints." *Theological Studies* 53 (1992): 517–33.

Deery, Joseph. *Our Lady of Lourdes.* Westminster, Md.: The Newman Press, 1958.

Dillard, Annie. *Pilgrim at Tinker Creek.* New York: Harper & Row, 1974.

Dossey, Larry. *Healing Words.* San Francisco: HarperCollins, 1993.

Dupre, Louis, and Don Saliers. *Christian Spirituality: Post-Reformation and Modern.* New York: Crossroads, 1989.

Dych, William V. "The Achievement of Karl Rahner." *Theology Digest* 31 (Winter 1984): 325–33.

———. *Karl Rahner.* Collegeville, Minn.: The Liturgical Press, 1992.

Edge, Hoyt. "Do Spirits Matter: Naturalism and Disembodied Survival." *Journal of the American Society for Psychical Research* 70 (1976): 290–302.

Egan, Harvey. *Christian Mysticism: The Future of a Tradition.* New York: Pueblo, 1984.

———. "The Devout Christian of the Future Will Be a 'Mystic.' Mysticism and Karl Rahner's Theology." In *Theology and Discovery: Essays in Honor of Karl Rahner,* edited by William J. Kelly, 139–58. Milwaukee: Marquette University Press, 1980.

———. *What Are They Saying About Mysticism?* New York/Mahwah, N.J.: Paulist Press, 1992.

Ehrenwald, Jan. "Precognition, Prophecy, and Self-fulfillment in Greco-Roman, Hebrew, and Aztec Antiquity." *International Journal of Parapsychology* (December 1967): 227–33.

———. "Precognition and the Prophetic Tradition." *Mystics and Medics*, edited by Reuven P. Bulka, 98–103. New York: Human Science Press, 1979.

Eliade, Mircea. *Patterns in Comparative Religion.* Translated by Rosemary Sheed. New York: Sheed & Ward, 1958.

———. *Rites and Symbols of Initiation.* Translated by Willard R. Trask. Putnam, Conn.: Spring Publications, 1958.

———. *Shamanism.* Translated by Edward R. Trask. Princeton, N.J.: Princeton University Press, 1972.

Epstein, Daniel Mark. *Sister Aimee: The Life of Aimee Semple McPherson.* New York: Harcourt Brace Jovanovich, Inc., 1993.

Epstein, Mark. *Going on Being: Buddhism and the Way of Change.* New York: Broadway Books, 2001.

Erikson, Erik. *Identity and the Life Cycle.* New York: W. W. Norton & Company, 1980.

Essman, Aaron H. "Visual Hallucinoses in Young Children." *The Psychological Study of the Child* 17 (1962): 334–43.

Eysenck, Hans J., and Carl Sargent. *Explaining the Unexplained.* London: Piron, 1993.

Farges, Albert. *Mystical Phenomena.* Translated by S. P. Jacques. London: Burns, Oates & Washbourne, Ltd., 1926.

Feinberg, Gerald. "Precognition—A Memory of Things Future." In *Quantum Physics and Parapsychology,* edited by Laura Oteri, 54–73. New York: Parapsychology Foundation, Inc., 1975.

Fodor, Nandor. "The Poltergeist—Psychoanalyzed." *Psychiatric Quarterly* 22 (1948): 195–203.

Frank, Jerome D. *Persuasion and Healing: A Comparative Study of Psychotherapy.* Baltimore: The Johns Hopkins University Press, 1961.

Frankl, Viktor. *Man's Search for Meaning.* New York: Washington Square Press, 1959.

Fransen, Peter. *The New Life of Grace.* New York: Seabury Press, 1973.

Freud, Anna. *The Ego and the Mechanisms of Defense.* Madison, Conn.: International Universities Press, Inc., 1966.

————. *Normality and Pathology in Childhood: Assessments of Development.* Madison, Conn.: International Universities Press, Inc., 1965.

Galton, Francis. "Statistical Inquiries into the Efficacy of Prayer." *Fortnightly Review* 12 (1872): 125–35.

Garnett, A. Campbell. "Matter, Mind, and Precognition." *Journal of Parapsychology* 29 (1965): 20–26.

Garrigou-Lagrange, Reginald. *Christian Perfection and Contemplation.* St. Louis: Herder, 1937.

Gauld, Alan, and Anthony D. Cornell. *Poltergeists.* London: Routledge & Keegan Paul, 1979.

Ghéon, Henri. *Secrets of the Saints.* Translated by F. J. Sheed. New York: Sheed & Ward, 1949.

Goldstein, Eda G. *Ego Psychology and Social Work Practice*, 2nd edition. New York: The Free Press, 1984.

Goodrich, Michael. *Violence and Miracle in the Fourteenth Century: Private Grief and Public Salvation.* Chicago: The University of Chicago Press, 1995.

Grad, Bernard. "Some Biological Effects of the 'Laying on of Hands': A Review of Experiments with Animals and Plants." *Journal of the American Society for Psychical Research* 49 (1965): 95–129.

———. "The 'Laying on of Hands': Implications for Psychotherapy, Gentling, and the Placebo Effect." *Journal of the Society for Psychical Research* 61 (1967): 286–305.

Greeley, Andrew M. *The Sociology of the Paranormal—A Reconnaissance.* Beverly Hills, Calif.: Sage Publications, 1975.

Green, Celia, and Charles McCreery. *Apparitions.* London: Hamish Hamilton Ltd., 1975.

Groeschel, Benedict J. *A Still, Small Voice.* San Francisco: Ignatius Press, 1993.

Guilbert, Joseph de. *The Theology of the Spiritual Life.* Translated by Paul Barrett. New York: Sheed & Ward, 1953.

Guiley, Rosemary. *Encyclopedia of Ghosts and Spirits.* New York: Checkmark Books, 2000.

———. *Encyclopedia of Mystical and Paranormal Experience.* New York: HarperCollins, 1991.

———. *Encyclopedia Saints.* New York: Checkmark Books, 2001.

Haight, Roger. *The Experience and Language of Grace.* New York: Paulist Press, 1979.

Hancock, Ann Marie. *Be a Light: Miracles at Medjugorje.* West Chester, Pa.: Whitford Press, 1988.

Happord, F. C. *Mysticism.* London: Penguin, 1963.

Haraldsson, Erlendur. *Modern Miracles.* New York: Hastings House, 1997.

———. "Psychokinetic Effects on Yeast: An Exploratory Experiment." In *Research in Parapsychology, 1972,* edited by R. L. Morris, William G. Roll, and J. D. Morris, 20–21. Metuchen, N.J.: Scarecrow Press, 1973.

Hardon, John A. "The Concept of Miracle from St. Augustine to Modern Apologetics." *Theological Studies* 15 (1954): 229–57.

Hart, Hornell. "Six Theories about Apparitions." *Proceedings of the Society for Psychical Research* 50 (May 1956): 153–239.

Haynes, Renée. "Miraculous and Paranormal Healing." *Parapsychology Review* 8 (September–October 1977): 25–28.

———. *Philosopher King.* London: Weidenfeld and Nicolson, 1970.

Heaney, John J. *The Sacred and the Psychic.* New York: Paulist Press, 1984.

Hebblethwaite, Brian, ed. *Divine Action.* Edinburgh: T. & T. Clark, 1990.

Hellé, Jean. *Miracles.* Translated by Lancelot C. Sheppard. New York: David McKay Company, 1952.

Heschel, Abraham. *The Prophets*, Vol. 1. New York: Harper and Row, 1962.

Hick, John. *An Interpretation of Religion: Human Responses to the Transcendent.* New Haven, Conn.: Yale University Press, 1989.

Honorton, Charles. "Meta-Analysis of Psi Ganzfeld Research: A Response to Hyman." *Journal of Parapsychology* 49 (1985): 51–91.

Honorton, Charles, and Diane Ferrari. "'Future Telling': A Meta-Analysis of Forced-Choice Precognition Experiments, 1935–1987." *Journal of Parapsychology* 53 (1989): 281–308.

Horney, Karen. *New Waves in Psychoanalysis.* New York: W. W. Norton & Company, 1939.

Idel, Moshe, and Bernard McGinn. *Mystical Union in Judaism, Christianity and Islam: An Ecumenical Dialogue.* New York: Crossroads, 1996.

Inglis, Brian. *Natural and Supernatural: A History of the Paranormal*. Garden City Park, N.Y.: Livery Publishing, 1992.

Irwin, Harvey J. *An Introduction to Parapsychology*. Jefferson, N.C.: McFarland & Company, 1989.

James, William. *The Varieties of Religious Experience*. New York: Longmans, Green, and Co., 1902.

John of the Cross, St. "Ascent of Mount Carmel." In *The Collected Works of St. John of the Cross*, rev. ed., translated by K. Kavanagh and O. Rodriguez, 113–349. Washington, D.C.: Institute of Carmelite Studies, 1991.

Johnson, Elizabeth A. "Does God Play Dice? Divine Providence and Chance." *Theological Studies* 57 (1996): 3–18.

———. "Marian Devotion in the Western Church." In *Christian Spirituality: High Middle Ages and Reformation*, edited by Jill Raitt, 392–414. New York: Crossroad Publishing, 1989.

Johnson, Kathleen. *Celestial Bodies*. New York: Pocket Books, 1987.

Johnston, William. *The Inner Eye of Love: Mysticism and Religion*. San Francisco: Harper & Row, 1978.

Joyce, C. R. B., and R. M. C. Weldon. "The Objective Efficacy of Prayer: A Double Blind Clinical Trial." *Journal of Chronic Disease* 18 (1965): 367–77.

Joyce, G. H. *The Question of Miracles*. London: The Manresa Press, 1914.

Jumi, Samuel. "Theoretical Foundations of Projection as a Defense Mechanism." *International Review of Psycho-Analysis* 6 (1979): 115–29.

Jung, Carl. *Psychology and Religion.* New Haven, Conn.: Yale University Press, 1938.

Kelsey, Morton. *The Christian and the Supernatural.* Minneapolis: Augsburg Publishing House, 1976.

———. *Discernment: A Study in Ecstacy and Evil.* New York: Paulist Press, 1978.

Kirkwood, Annie. *Mary's Message to the World.* London: Piatkus, 1995.

Laurentin, Réne. *Bernadette of Lourdes.* Translated by John Drury. Minneapolis: Winston Press, 1979.

Lawrence, Tony R. "How Many Factors of Paranormal Belief Are There?" *Journal of Parapsychology* 59 (1995): 3–25.

LeShan, Lawrence. *The Medium, the Mystic, and the Physicist.* London: Turnstone Books, 1966.

Lewis, C. S. *Miracles.* New York: Macmillan, 1947.

Lewis, I. M. *Ecstatic Religion,* 2nd ed. London: Routledge, 1989.

Marchand, A. *The Facts of Lourdes and the Medical Bureau.* Translated by Dom Francis Izard. London: Burns, Oates & Washbourne, Ltd., 1924.

Martindale, C. C. *The Meaning of Fatima.* New York: P. J. Kenedy & Sons, 1950.

McBrien, Richard. *Catholicism.* San Francisco: HarperCollins, 1981.

McClure, Kevin. *The Evidence for the Visions of the Virgin Mary.* Wellingborough, England: The Aquarian Press, 1983.

McGinn, Bernard. *The Flowering of Mysticism.* New York: Crossroads, 1998.

———. *The Foundations of Mysticism.* New York: Crossroads, 1991.

———. *The Growth of Mysticism.* New York: Crossroads, 1994.

McGinn, Bernard, and John Meyendorff. *Christian Spirituality: Origins to the Twelfth Century*. New York: Crossroads, 1988.

McKenna, Briege, with Henry Libersat. *Miracles Do Happen*. New York: St. Martin's Press, 1988.

McMahon, Joanne D. S. "Physiological Correlates of Religious Belief and Psychical Research: Decomposition and You." Proceedings of the 24th Annual Conference of the Academy of Religion and Psychical Research. Held at the Ramada Inn, Philadelphia International Airport, Essington, Pa., June 4–6, 1999.

McMahon, Joanne D. S., and Anna Lascurain. *Shopping for Miracles: A Guide to Psychics and Psychical Powers*. Roxbury Park, Calif.: Lowell House, 1997.

Melinsky, M. A. H. *Healing Miracles*. London: A. R. Mowbray & Co., Ltd., 1968.

Merton, Thomas. *New Seeds of Contemplation*. New York: New Directions, 1962.

Mertz, Lisa. "The Spirits Say They Aren't Crazy: Trance and Healing in Cultural Context." *ReVision* 17 (September 1994): 29–34.

Mims, Cedric. *When We Die: The Science, Culture, and Rituals of Death*. New York: St. Martin's Griffin, 1999.

Miravalle, Mark I. *The Message of Medjugorje*. Lanham, Md.: University Press of America, 1986.

Monden, Louis. *Signs and Wonders*. New York: Desclee Company, 1966.

Morris, Robert L. "Assessing Experimental Support for True Precognition." *Journal of Parapsychology* 46 (1982): 321–36.

Moyers, Bill. *Healing and the Mind*. New York: Doubleday, 1993.

Mundle, C. W. K. "Does the Concept of Precognition Make Sense?" *International Journal of Parapsychology* 4 (1964): 180–94.

Murphy, Gardner. *The Challenge of Psychical Research.* New York: Harper & Row, 1961.

———. "Direct Contacts with Past and Future: Retrocognition and Precognition." *Journal of the American Society for Psychical Research* 61 (1967): 3–23.

Nash, Carroll B. "Test of Psychokinetic Control of Bacterial Mutation." *Journal of the American Society for Psychical Research* 78 (1984): 145–52.

Nickell, Joe. *Looking for a Miracle.* Buffalo, N.Y.: Prometheus Books, 1993.

Nielsson, Haraldur. "Remarkable Psychic Phenomena in Iceland." *Journal of the American Society for Psychical Research* (1924): 233–38.

O'Donovan, Leo J. "A Journey into Time: The Legacy of Karl Rahner's Last Years." *Theological Studies* 46 (1985): 621–46.

———, ed. *A World of Grace.* New York: Crossroad Publishing, 1989.

Omez, Reginald. *Psychical Phenomena.* Translated by Renée Haynes. New York: Hawthorn Books, 1958.

Orme, J. E. "Precognition and Time." *Journal of the Society for Psychical Research* 47 (1974): 351–65.

Otto, Rudolf. *The Idea of the Holy.* Translated by John Harvey. New York: Oxford University Press, 1981.

Palmer, John. "A Community Mall Survey of Psychic Experiences." *Journal of the American Society for Psychical Research* 73 (1979): 221–51.

————. "Extrasensory Perception: Research Findings." In *Advances in Parapsychological Research*, edited by Stanley Krippner, 71–81. New York: Plenum Press, 1978.

Palmer, John, and Richard Broughton. "An Updated Meta-Analysis of Post-PRL ESP Ganzfeld Experiments." *Proceedings of Presented Papers: The Parapsychological Association 43rd Annual Convention* (2000): 224–40.

Pelletier, Joseph A. *The Queen of Peace Visits Medjugorje.* Worcester, Mass.: Assumption Publications, 1985.

Pert, Candace. *Molecules of Emotion.* New York: Touchstone Press, 1997.

Poulain, Augustin. *The Graces of Interior Prayer.* Translated from the sixth edition by Lenora L. Yorke Smith. London: Routledge & Kegan Paul Ltd., 1950.

Radin, Dean, and Roger D. Nelson. "Consciousness-Related Effects in Random Physical Systems." *Foundations of Physics* 19 (1989): 1499–1514.

Rahner, Karl. "Christian Living Formerly and Today." *Theological Investigations, Vol. 7: Further Theology of the Spiritual Life*, translated by David Burke, 3–24. New York: Herder and Herder, 1971.

————. "Christology Within an Evolutionary View." *Theological Investigations, Vol. 5: Later Writings*, translated by Karl H. Kruger, 157–92. London: Darton, Longman and Todd, 1966.

————. "The Concept of Mystery in Catholic Theology," "Nature and Grace," "Theology of Symbol." *Theological Investigations, Vol. 4: More Recent Writings*, translated by Kevin Smyth, 36–73, 165–88, 221–52. London: Darton, Longman and Todd, 1966.

———. "Concerning the Relationship Between Nature and Grace." *Theological Investigations, Vol. 1: God, Christ, Mary and Grace*, translated by Cornelius Ernst, 297–317. London: Darton, Longman and Todd, 1961.

———. *The Dynamic Element in the Church*. Translated by W. J. O'Hara. New York: Herder and Herder, 1964.

———. *Everyday Faith*. Translated by W. J. O'Hara. New York: Herder and Herder, 1968.

———. "Experience of the Spirit and Existential Commitment," "Religious Enthusiasm and the Experience of Grace," "The 'Spiritual Senses' According to Origen," "The Doctrine of the 'Spiritual Senses' in the Middle Ages." *Theological Investigations, Vol. 16: Experience of the Spirit: Source of Theology*, translated by David Morland, 24–34, 35–51, 81–103, 104–34. London: Darton, Longman and Todd, 1979.

———. "Experience of Transcendence from the Standpoint of Catholic Dogmatics." *Theological Investigations, Vol. 18: God and Revelation*, translated by Edward Quinn, 173–88. New York: Crossroad Publishing, 1983.

———. *Faith in a Wintry Season: Conversations and Interviews with Karl Rahner in the Last Years of His Life*. Edited by Paul Imhof and Hubert Biallowons. Translation edited by Harvey D. Egan. New York: Crossroad Publishing, 1990.

———. *Foundations of Christian Faith*. Translated by William V. Dych. New York: Seabury Press, 1978.

———. *Hearers of the Word*. Translated by Michael Richards. New York: Herder and Herder, 1969.

———. *Hominisation: The Evolutionary Origin of Man as a Theological Problem*. Translated by W. J. O'Hara. New York: Herder and Herder, 1965.

————. *Karl Rahner in Dialogue.* Edited by Paul Imhof and Hubert Biallowans. Translation edited by Harvey D. Egan. New York: Crossroad Publishing, 1986.

————. "Mystical Experience and Mystical Theology." *Theological Investigations, Vol. 17: Jesus, Man, and the Church,* translated by Margaret Kohl, 90–99. London: Darton, Longman and Todd, 1979.

————. "Mysticism." In *Encyclopedia of Theology,* edited by Karl Rahner, 1010–11. New York: Seabury Press, 1975.

————. *Opportunities for Faith.* Translated by Edward Quinn. New York: Seabury Press, 1970.

————. *The Practice of Faith.* Edited by Karl Lehman and Albert Raffelt. New York: Crossroad Publishing, 1986.

————. *On Prayer.* Collegeville, Minn.: Liturgical Press, 1958.

————. "Reflections on the Gradual Ascent to Christian Perfection," "Reflections on the Experience of Grace," "The Ignatian Mysticism of Joy in the World," "Some Theses for a Devotion to the Sacred Heart." *Theological Investigations, Vol. 3: The Theology of the Spiritual Life,* translated by Karl H. Kruger and Boniface Kruger, 3–23, 86–90, 277–93, 331–52. London: Darton, Longman and Todd, 1967.

————. "The Relationship Between Theology and Popular Religion." *Theological Investigations, Vol. 22: Human Society and the Church of Tomorrow,* translated by Joseph Donceel, 140–47. New York: Crossroad Publishing, 1991.

————. *Visions and Prophecies.* Translated by Charles Henkey and Richard Strachan. New York: Herder and Herder, 1963. (Original work published 1958.)

Rahner, Karl, and Herbert Vorgrimler. *Dictionary of Theology*, 2nd ed., translated by Richard Strachan. New York: Crossroad Publishing, 1981.

Raitt, Jill. *Christian Spirituality: High Middle Ages and Reformation*. New York: Crossroads, 1989.

Rein, Glen. "A Psychokinetic Effect on Neurotransmitter Metabolism: Alterations in the Degradative Enzyme Monoamie Oxidase." *Parapsychological Association Presentation of Papers* 2 (1985): 235–44.

Rilke, Rainer Maria. *The Notebooks of Malte Laurids Brigge*. Translated by Stephen Mitchell. New York: Vintage Books, 1990).

Rogo, D. Scott. *An Experience of Phantoms*. New York: Taplinger Publishing Company, 1974.

———. *Miracles*. New York: Dial Press, 1982.

———. *Parapsychology: A Century of Inquiry*. New York: Taplinger Publishing Company, 1975.

Roll, William G. "Towards a General Theory for the Poltergeist." *European Journal of Parapsycholgy* (1978): 167–200.

———. *The Poltergeist*. Metuchen, N.J.: Scarecrow Press, 1976.

Ryan, Maurice. "Fatima, Lourdes, and Medjugorje: A Challenge for Religious Educators." *Religious Education* 88 (1993): 564–75.

Sacks, Oliver. *The Man Who Mistook His Wife for a Hat*. New York: Harper & Row, 1987.

Santos, Lucia. *Fatima in Lucia's Own Words: Sister Lucia's Memoirs*, 8th ed. Translated by Dominican Nuns of Perpetual Rosary. Still River, Mass.: Ravensgate Press, 1989.

Seward, Desmond. *The Dancing Sun*. London: Macmillan, 1993.

Smith, Robert D. *Comparative Miracles*. New York: B. Herder Book Co., 1965.

Solfvin, Jerry. "Mutual Healing." *Advances in Parapsychological Research*, edited by Stanley Krippner, 31–63. Jefferson, N.C.: McFarland & Company, 1984.

Spiegel, David. "Effects of Psychosocial Support on Patients with Metastatic Breast Cancer." *Journal of Psychosocial Oncology* 10 (1992): 113–20.

Stefano, P., and M. Manelli. *Short Story of a Victim: Theresa Musco [1943-1976]*. Translated by Joanna Pearson. S. Mari, Italy: Eitrice Terzo Millennio, 1984.

Stevenson, Ian. "Are Poltergeists Living or Are They Dead?" *Journal of the American Society for Psychical Research* 66 (1972): 233–52.

———. "Survival After Death." In *Psychical Research: A Guide to Its History, Principles and Practices*, edited by Ivor Grattan-Guiness, 109–22. Wellingborough, England: Aquarian Press, 1982.

Swinburne, Richard, ed. *Miracles*. New York: Macmillan, 1989.

———. *Revelation*. Oxford: Clarendon Press, 1992.

Tanquerey, Adolphe. *The Spiritual Life*. Translated by Herman Branderis. Belgium: Desclée & Co., 1930.

Tart, Charles, ed. "Information Acquisition Rates in Forced-Choice ESP Experiments: Precognition Does Not Work as Well as Present-Time ESP." *Journal of the American Society for Psychical Research* 77 (1983): 293–310.

———. *Transpersonal Psychologies*. San Francisco: Harper & Row, 1975.

Teilhard de Chardin, Pierre. *Christianity and Evolution.* Translated by René Hague. New York: Harcourt Brace Jovanovich, Inc., 1971.

Teresa of Avila, St. *The Life of Saint Teresa of Avila by Herself.* Translated by J. M. Cohen. London: Penguin, 1957.

Thomas, Owen C., ed. *God's Activity in the World.* Atlanta: Scholars Press, 1983.

Thouless, R. H., and B. P. Weisner. "The Psi Processes in Normal and 'Paranormal' Psychology." *Proceedings of the Society of Psychical Research* 48 (1948): 177–96.

Thurston, Herbert. *The Physical Phenomena of Mysticism.* Edited by J. H. Crehan. Chicago: Henry Regnery Company, 1952.

Tyrrell, G. N. M. *Apparitions.* London: Duckworth & Co., 1942.

Underhill, Evelyn. *Mysticism.* New York: E. P. Dutton and Co., 1954.

Utts, Jessica. "An Assessment of the Evidence for Psychic Functioning." *Journal of Scientific Exploration* 10 (1996): 3–30.

Van Dam, Raymond. *Saints and Their Miracles in Late Antique Gaul.* Princeton, N.J.: Princeton University Press, 1993.

Vasiliev, L. L. *Experiements in Distant Influence.* New York: E. P. Dutton & Company, 1962.

Volken, Laurent. *Visions, Revelations and the Church.* Translated by Edward Gallagher. New York: P. J. Kenedy & Sons, 1963.

Vorgrimler, Herbert. *Karl Rahner.* Translated by Edward Quinn. London: Burns & Oates Ltd., 1965.

Walsh, James, ed. *The Cloud of Unknowing.* Mahwah, N.J.: Paulist Press, 1981.

Walsh, William Thomas. *Our Lady of Fatima*. New York: Doubleday, 1954.

Ward, Benedicta. *Miracles and the Medieval Mind*. Philadelphia: University of Pennsylvania Press, 1982.

Ward, Keith. *Divine Action*. London: Collins Publishing, 1990.

———. *A Vision to Pursue*. London: SCM Press, 1991.

Warner, Marina. "Blood and Tears." *The New Yorker* (April 8, 1996): 63–69.

Watkins, Graham K., and Anita M. Watkins "Possible PK Influence on the Resuscitation of Anesthetized Mice." *Journal of Parapsychology* 35 (1971): 257–72.

Weill, Andrew. *Health and Healing*. Boston: Houghton Mifflin Company, 1988.

Wells, Roger, and Judith Klein. "A Replication of 'Psychic Healing' Paradigm." *Journal of Parapsychology* 36 (1972): 144–50.

Wells, Roger, and Graham K. Watkins, "Linger Effect in Several PK Experiments." In *Research in Parapsychology 1974*, edited by J. D. Morris. Metuchen, N.J.: Scarecrow Press, 1975.

West, Donald J. *Eleven Lourdes Miracles*. London: Gerald Duckworth & Co., 1957.

White, Victor. *God and the Unconscious*. Chicago: H. Regnery Co., 1953.

Woods, Richard, ed. *Understanding Mysticism*. London: Athalone Press, 1980.

Woodward, Kenneth L. *Making Saints*. New York: Simon & Schuster, 1990.

Zimdars-Swartz, Sandra L. *Encountering Mary: From La Salette to Medjugorje*. Princeton: Princeton University Press, 1991.